H75$ 975

Doyle
Reis

I0292015

MICROCOUNSELING

Foreword by

Robert R. Carkhuff, Ph.D.

Professor of Psychology and Education
Director, Center for Human Relations and Community Affairs
American International College
Springfield, Massachusetts

Introduction by

Dwight W. Allen, Ed.D.

Dean, School of Education
University of Massachusetts
Amherst, Massachusetts

Fourth Printing

MICROCOUNSELING

Innovations in Interviewing Training

By

ALLEN E. IVEY

Human Relations Center
University of Massachusetts
Amherst, Massachusetts

With a Contribution by

John R. Moreland

Oklahoma City Veterans Administration Hospital and
the University of Oklahoma Medical School
Oklahoma City, Oklahoma

CHARLES C THOMAS · PUBLISHER
Springfield · Illinois · U.S.A.

Published and Distributed Throughout the World by

CHARLES C THOMAS • PUBLISHER

BANNERSTONE HOUSE

301-327 East Lawrence Avenue, Springfield, Illinois, U.S.A.

This book is protected by copyright. No part of it may be reproduced in any manner without written permission from the publisher.

© *1971 by* CHARLES C THOMAS • PUBLISHER

ISBN 0-398-02323-9

Library of Congress Catalog Card Number: 75-157287

First Printing, 1971
Second Printing, 1972
Third Printing, 1974
Fourth Printing, 1975

With THOMAS BOOKS *careful attention is given to all details of manufacturing and design. It is the Publisher's desire to present books that are satisfactory as to their physical qualities and artistic possibilities and appropriate for their particular use.* THOMAS BOOKS *will be true to those laws of quality that assure a good name and good will.*

Printed in the United States of America

N-1

To   Betty
             Billy and John
             My parents

FOREWORD

MICROTRAINING IS Allen Ivey's innovative answer to the need
for developing counselor behaviors which are helpful to the
client. A structural or methodological approach, microtraining
attempts first to identify specific counselor behaviors and then
to systematically train the counselor-candidate in these behaviors.
Based upon the concept of microteaching developed by Allen and
his colleagues, microtraining utilizes a "shaping" process involving immediate and concrete feedback, primarily from a videotaping of a brief counselor-client interaction.

Microtraining has demonstrated its usefulness in facilitating
counselor learning of effective techniques and in minimizing the
risk to both counselor and client over the course of the .training
experience. Indeed, there is some tentative evidence to suggest
direct client benefits in the form of increased client participation
and positive client feedback. Although I am reluctant to rely
heavily upon the perceptions of clients due to the interpersonal
distortions inherent in the nature of their problems, there is
extensive evidence to indicate that different indexes of client
process involvement are related to a variety of client outcome
measures. The client cannot utilize the counseling experience
most effectively if he does not participate in it. The counselor
cannot be helpful if the client does not share his problems with
him at some behavioral level, verbal or otherwise.

In this context, Ivey's concepts of "intentional counselors"
offering specific "attending behaviors" in order to involve the
client in a process leading to the behavior change or gain of the
client are most useful. The trainee actually practices the skills
which the training program is calculated to effect—a most unusual
practice in counselor education! The training outcome indexes
do in fact reflect the training program.

What intrigues me most about the concept of microtraining

is its potential relationship to my own developing theme of "training as a preferred mode of treatment." Just as we can train counselor-candidates in a systematic way to demonstrate helpful behaviors so also can we train clients in useful behaviors. To be sure, the training for the client would take place most facilitatively in the context of an atmosphere of understanding and regard. Without such responsive relationship conditions, the client's self-exploration and self-understanding which is necessary to determine behavioral goals that would be useful to him would not be possible. However, I would emphasize that in the context of a facilitative relationship, the counselor can most effectively accomplish the ends of counseling—*tangible client benefits as determined by the client's needs*—by systematic training similar to that advocated by Ivey. The approach which is most effective for counselors is also most effective for clients. In my own terms, the business of counseling is one of transforming helpees into helpers, and it is the counselor-trainer's task to utilize the most effective means for accomplishing this, whether the helpees are counselor-trainees or clients. Indeed, the helpees can be most efficiently transformed into helpers by training them directly in helper's skills.

Perhaps another important contribution of microtraining is its potential for cutting, rather than unraveling, the Gordian knot of meaning versus rigor. It is not a question of experiential or operational, or training or spontaneity. Systematic training provides the response repertoire without which an individual cannot be spontaneous. The counseling field has lived too long with mutually exclusive, artificial dichotomies perpetrated by those who are proficient in none of the alternatives which they propose. Ivey's microtraining approach provides the opportunity for making the experiential operational, for systematizing both what is experientially true and empirically validated.

In this context, where an innovator "is coming from" is critical. It is my own belief that all science begins with the sensory experience of the scientist. Rather than take it for granted, the perception of the perceiver must be studied. It is his personal phenomenology that dictates the perseverance, in spite of repeated failures, of an Einstein or a Freud or a Skinner.

In this instance, Ivey is coming from a very broad and eclectic frame of reference and filling in the details of the model from the data of basic researchers. This contrasts which much of the work in psychology and education, which comes from a relatively narrow frame of reference and is then extended on a broad front to attempt to account for phenomena that extend beyond the workers' limits.

Indeed, just as Ivey's counselor-trainees benefit most from an approach integrating the unique contributions of all positions, so also do we find our most effective contributors in psychology and education demonstrating high levels of expertise in all relevant areas; those who are most expert in the issues of meaning are most expert in the issues of rigor and vice versa. In counseling, a counselor cannot term his effort effective until he has made systematic inquiries into his effects upon the client's behavior. Similarly, a counselor cannot call himself rigorous until he has experienced the complexities of the process of human behavior change. The effects of counseling upon client behavior cannot be maximized until the contributions of both meaning and rigor are integrated into an effective training experience.

Ivey has accomplished this integration of meaning and rigor in his directional yet open-ended approach to counselor training. Microtraining is not simply a useful technique. *It is a preferred technique of skills acquisition,* for it is based upon the principle of practicing that which we wish to effect.

In summary, Ivey's eclectic effort represents a significant contribution to the counseling literature. Its statement is clear and straightforward. It should be read by all those counselor educators and candidates who are concerned with the translation of their efforts into tangible human benefits.

ROBERT R. CARKHUFF

INTRODUCTION

MICROCOUNSELING AND ITS EDUCATIONAL IMPLICATIONS

Microteaching was designed as a new approach to teaching specific classroom instructional skills. In the early phases of experimentation and research, conceptual frameworks and theoretical constructs were deliberately omitted in a search for a method which consistently showed results—a system that "worked" was needed rather than one which was theoretically sophisticated. Our belief was that a theoretical structure for microteaching would evolve out of application and practice.

The publication of *Microcounseling: Innovations in Interviewing Techniques* brings the microtraining paradigm to a new level which illustrates even more clearly its adaptability in an almost infinite variety of training situations. Although focusing primarily on interviewing and counseling skills, Allen Ivey has produced a set of constructs and conceptualized them so that they will be valuable in many other settings beyond the interview. In addition, he clearly describes the process of skill development and suggests a variety of means through which the microtraining paradigm may be adapted in other settings. The microtraining paradigm has now been employed in training settings as diverse as psychotherapy, firefighting, dentistry, speech therapy, and personnel interviewing. This seems only the beginning.

Perhaps the most important implication of Ivey's work is his emphasis on using microtraining to teach individuals the "developmental skills of being people." Our society has been too concerned with imparting content or knowledge skills; we are now faced with a society that is unable to understand and relate with itself. The feasibility of identifying and teaching specific skills of human relations has been demonstrated by Ivey and his colleagues. The next logical step would appear to be development of "human relations learning units" which could be utilized in schools and governmental and business institutions to facilitate the process of personal growth and humanizing our society.

On another level, special note should be taken of Ivey's use of the construct of "attending behavior." While attention and related constructs are emphasized in both behavioral and existential literature, they have not generally been used as a training focus. Attending behavior and its related constructs may be a central dimension not only for interviewing training but also for the teaching and learning processes. I am also impressed by Ivey's interest in reconciling the supposed differences in behavioral and existential psychology. It has long been my belief that these views simply represent two of a variety of different symbolic language systems of life's experience. The discussion in Chapter Three provides a good framework for discussion and examination of these two supposedly different views of man. Perhaps they are not that distant after all.

Microteaching until now has focused primarily on what Ivey would term "self-expression skills." He has developed another role for the teacher which has not been fully stressed in microteaching to date—the role of the teacher as listener, as facilitator to the growth of students. There is need for teachers to learn listening skills, such as attending and reflection of feeling, if they are to understand pupils and help them become more fully human. Hopefully this is a prelude to other roles and perspectives for the preparation of teachers.

Microteaching and microcounseling may now best be conceptualized within the larger paradigm of microtraining—a systematic method of skills acquisition designed to equip the individual not only with tools but also with the freedom to be human. Microtraining has demonstrated its utility far beyond our original work with teachers at Stanford University. I anticipate a time when the microtraining paradigm helps us see more clearly the relationships between the teaching and counseling processes, sales training and interviewing, and training couples in effective marital communication and psychotherapy.

Clearly, work on microtraining and its many possibilities is only beginning. We have only preliminary evidence on such important issues as generalization of skills from training, which aspects of the microtraining paradigm are most important to which individuals, and interrelationships between supposedly different areas of study such as speech therapy and teaching social studies. It is my anticipation that further research and experimentation within the microtraining paradigm will lead to new syntheses of skill development. I visualize a time when teachers, social workers, therapists, and human beings will have as a regular part of their educational experience regular instruction in skills of effective communication. Further, it is my expectation that this instruction will include not only the formal microtraining paradigm but also a wide variety of adaptations.

Microtraining is best considered a beginning, a "jumping-off" point from which each individual or group of individuals develop their own conceptions and directions for further growth. I have found that the innovation is most effective when someone can reshape it and use it in their own style. Microtraining is an innovation that each individual can use in his own way and make important and unique contributions not only to others but also to his own personal growth.

With Allen Ivey, I would like to commend a new view toward microteaching and microcounseling. Rather than using these procedures in a set, prescribed manner, experiment and develop microtraining in your own unique fashion.

I hope you find a way to use microcounseling techniques to develop new approaches, as a stimulus to new mechanisms of microtraining and not simply as a recipe for a narrow range of counseling and interviewing skills. To go beyond Ivey's ideas— to make them obsolete as he has in part made other ideas obsolete by amplificating the earlier efforts in microteaching— is one ultimate compliment you can give his work.

DWIGHT W. ALLEN

ACKNOWLEDGMENTS

M ICROCOUNSELING, AS MOST other innovations, rests heavily on the work and support of many individuals. Some see innovation as appearing spontaneously without history; not being one who believes that anything is created out of nothing, I would like to recognize and express my appreciation to those who made this work possible.

Dwight Allen, Dean of the School of Education, University of Massachusetts, completed extensive work in microteaching at Stanford University, which provided the foundation from which this project began. Edward Brainard of the Charles F. Kettering Foundation (now at CFK Limited, Denver) provided the link for financial support for microcounseling development and extensive personal support in the early phases of this project. Without these two men, microcounseling would not have seen the light of day.

Development and implementation of the microcounseling model, however, rested first with the research team at Colorado State University in 1966 to 1968. The development of the concept of attending behavior is an example of how we had worked together in developing this method. Six months into the project, discouraged with our progress to date, Weston Morrill suggested that we try to train our secretary in counseling. As he and I worked with her, we originated the key concepts underlying much of this book in about twenty minutes. Relaxed and happy with the success we had met, we still did not have a name which fit the concept; I still remember Dean Miller looking up from his desk and saying "Why not call the behavioral complex attending behavior?" Cheryl Normington carried the concept further with her development of the reflection-of-feeling study. Richard Haase provided general administrative support, developed instruments, and was an invaluable participant. He has since completed important independent work on the topic at the University of Massachusetts. All of the team has continued their involvement with microcounseling and have played key roles in the development of new skills and methods within this framework.

I arrived at the University of Massachusetts in 1968 and found Jeanne Phillips, John Moreland, and Jeff Lockhart as stimulating colleagues. The work and thinking of these three people in the final development of the concepts presented in this book are central. Many of the skills discussed in Chapter Four come from their work or were suggested by conversations with them.

Several graduate students contributed much to microcounseling as colleagues, through dissertations and work on special projects as graduate assistants. Edward Aldrige, Thomas Crowley, Richard Hackney, William Higgins, Joyce Hinckley, Stephen Rollin, Max Uhlemann, and Shem Zeevi made substantial and substantive contributions to the development of microcounseling.

In relation to important research and adaptations of microcounseling presented in this book, I would like to express my admiration and appreciation to Martin Bloom, Elizabeth Collins, David Cowles, Stephen Danish, Dominic DiMattia, Leonard Donk, Mark Frankel, Warren Freiband, Elizabeth Goldberg, David Greenall, John Hinkle, Gilbert Hutchcraft, Ruth Becky Irwin, Elsworth Keil, Jan Kelley, Daniel Malamud, Sy Rudman, Andrew Schwebel, Thomas Thielen, and George Wawrykow.

Eugene Oetting, Charles Cole, and Burns Crookston of Colorado State University must be recognized as individuals without whom this work would not have been possible. Their constant admonitions, criticisms, and support provided much of the underlying basis for the ideas expressed here. It must also be recalled that Thomas Magoon of the University of Maryland was talking about innovation in counseling before I even knew what the concept could mean. David Danskin of Kansas State University, always willing to go out on a limb with a wild idea, helped me develop a more creative and playful approach to human behavior change. Jerry Jacobson should also be recognized for his invaluable training in flexible and creative thinking processes. David Tiedeman of Harvard provided a constant model of excellence and a vision of a higher goal.

Robert Carkhuff of American International College is es pecially recognized for his innovative work in facilitating human relations. His ideas were most helpful in developing the concepts discussed in this book.

It should be noted that the microtraining project was initiated under a grant from the Charles F. Kettering Foundation. I am grateful for their support and interest.

I give special thanks to Jeanne Drwila, Carole Wheeler, and Ruth Edwards for typing and criticizing innumerable drafts about the same topic. I am sure they are glad to see this project completed.

The manuals presented in Appendix A are the combined work of many people. They have been rewritten and reworked many times so that it is now difficult to say who was most involved in the development of each skill. Recognizing this difficulty, the following individuals were involved in the development of the specific skills:

1. Attending behavior, reflection of feeling, and summarization of feeling—Cheryl Normington, Weston Morrill, Richard Haase, C. Dean Miller.
2. Selective attention to client's attitudes toward tests— C. Dean Miller, Weston Morrill, Cheryl Normington, Max Uhlemann.
3. Open invitation to talk, minimal encourages, paraphrasing and summarization—Jeanne Phillips, John Moreland, Jeff Lockhart.
4. Direct, mutual communication—William Higgins, Max Uhlemann.
5. Expression of feeling—Richard Haase, Douglas Forsyth, Mary Alice Guttman, R. Lee.
6. Interpretation—John Moreland.

Appreciation is expressed to the Macmillan Company for permission to reprint an extended quote from a paper by Daniel Malamud taken from *Encounter: Confrontations in Self and Interpersonal Awareness* edited by L. Blank, G. Gottsegen, and

M. Gottsegen to be published in 1971. Holt, Rinehart, and Winston gave permission for a short selection from R. R. Carkhuff's *Helping and Human Relations* Vol. II (1969) to be reprinted here. Three articles from the *Journal of Counseling Psychology* published by the American Psychological Association formed the basis for much of the thinking of this book and with permission portions appear throughout (Ivey, Normington, Miller, Morrill, and Haase, 1968; Higgins, Ivey, and Uhlemann, 1970; Hackney, Ivey, and Oetting, 1970).

CONTENTS

MICROCOUNSELING

Chapter One

MICROTRAINING AND MICROCOUNSELING: DEFINITION AND PROMISE

A YOUNG MAN IS talking intently about his attitudes toward a recent job; a novice interviewer appears to be listening closely. With some heat and emotion, the young man tells about a conflict with his superior. The interviewer does not respond and an awkward pause occurs. The interviewer shifts uncomfortably in his chair and asks his client what some of his objectives in his next position might be. A supervisor is recording the session with a portable videotape recorder and takes notes on the novice's and the client's behavior.

Shortly after, the session is terminated, and the young man completes an evaluation form and leaves the room. The supervisor and the interviewing trainee discuss the session, examine the client evaluation form, and view parts of the videotaped session. The client is then interviewed again and the process of recording and feedback is repeated. In the second session, the novice interviewer appears more relaxed and able to listen. When the conflict with the superior again appears, the trainee listens more fully to the client and does not shift topics when emotions appear. The client is able to express his attitudes and hopes more fully.

This process, a scaled-down interviewing session, is microcounseling. In such microtraining techniques, a beginning counselor talks with a volunteer client about real problems. The interview occurs in a setting which provides interviewing practice with maximum opportunity for immediate feedback and trainee growth. The compressed nature of the situation allows a focus on specific dimensions of interviewing skills and does not demand

3

that the trainee respond immediately as a fully professional counselor.

Microtraining may be compared to the traditional approach to interviewing training in which the beginning interviewer, counselor, or therapist is quite literally "thrown in" to his first session with a long list of caveats, concepts, and suggested methods. He is expected to sort all this information and act effectively. Teaching beginning counselors and therapists how to counsel is one of the more complex and challenging issues facing counseling (Krumboltz, 1967; Matarazzo, Wiens, and Saslow, 1966; Wrenn, 1962). Most would agree that counselor and interviewer training have not generally been efficient or economical of human resources. Beginning interviewers often find their first sessions confusing. They frequenty have trouble in defining their own role in the interview and in getting the client to talk.

In effect, microcounseling provides an opportunity for those who are preparing to counsel to obtain a liberal amount of practice without endangering or offending clients. While microtraining has other possible purposes and uses, its principal aim is to provide experiences which serve as a bridge between classroom or textbook theory and actual practice in interviewing and counseling. Too many enter the counseling and interviewing fields without supervised practice in interviewing skills.

MICROTRAINING: A STRUCTURAL INNOVATION

Cartwright (1968), in a review of psychotherapy research, singled out the educational process for training novice clinicians as being in particular need of systematic study. Instruction in basic clinical and interviewing skills is carried out in educational institutions with students preparing for many professions, including psychological and educational counseling, medicine, nursing, psychiatry, clinical psychology, the ministry, and subprofessional helping roles. Industry and the United States Employment Service are greatly concerned with interviewing and have given considerable thought to methods of improving training in this field.

Microcounseling and microtraining techniques are a direct attempt to develop a systematic approach to interviewing training. Although not attempting to answer all the questions about interviewing or counseling, the microtraining framework does suggest interview techniques which can be studied and taught more systematically than had previously been thought.

Microtraining techniques should be considered as a *structural or methodological approach* to interviewing training. The skeleton or structure of microcounseling gives one a framework for a relatively precise behavioral skill of counseling, shortens interview length, and provides intensive practice until a skill is learned thoroughly. Video or other types of feedback techniques provide important support for learning within the microcounseling structure.

This relatively simple model could be applied to virtually every skill area of human endeavor. Microtraining techniques have been or could be applied to firefighting skills, salesmanship, or the most complex skills of human interaction. Regardless of the level or complexity of the skill taught, the microtraining framework of interview-training-reinterview remains constant.

A structural innovation such as microcounseling provides a framework which can be used to solve many types of problems in skill training. The program helps one to systematically break down a behavior which needs to be taught and then supports effective instruction in this same skill. Microtraining techniques can be used to teach individuals who have widely diverse areas of expertise or interest. These procedures may be used to train subprofessionals in elementary skills of counseling and interviewing; or at another level, they may be used to teach advanced clinicians specific clinical skills or to train high-level executives in aspects of successful supervision.

In this book, the words "interviewing," "counseling," and "therapy" will be used interchangeably. We define *interviewing* as a process of information seeking (most typically in a personnel or placement situation); *counseling* as seeking to understand another person more fully (school guidance, college counseling); and *therapy* as helping another person change pathological behavior (analysis, long-term treatment, behavior modification).

Despite these differences, all interviewers, counselors, and therapists must learn to listen, to ask questions, to attend to feelings,
and to interpret their clients' statements. Therefore, the skills
outlined in this book should be useful to those who work with
people in many settings.

THE BASIC MICROCOUNSELING MODEL

While many variations are possible, most research and
methodology in microcounseling has been conducted in a situation in which the trainee goes through the following progressive
steps:

1. The trainee receives instructions to enter a room where
   he will interview a client. Depending on the situation,
   the topic may or may not be defined. Similar instructions
   are given to the volunteer client, with the exception that
   he is told he is about to be interviewed.
2. A five-minute diagnostic session (with the trainee interviewing the client) is then videotaped.
3. The client leaves the room and completes an evaluation
   form or may be interviewed by a second supervisor.
   These data are then available for the supervisory session
   with the trainee.
4. The trainee reads a written manual describing the specific
   skill to be learned in this session. The supervisor talks
   with him about the session and about the manual.
5. Video models of an expert demonstrating the specific
   skill are shown. There may be a positive and a negative
   model of the skill.
6. The trainee is shown his initial interview and discusses
   this with his supervisor. He is asked to identify examples
   where he engaged in or failed to apply the specific skill
   in question.
7. The supervisor and trainee review the skill together and
   plan for the next counseling session.
8. The trainee reinterviews the same client for five minutes.
9. Feedback and evaluation on the final session are made
   available to the trainee.

It may be observed that the training procedures involve cue

discrimination and specific suggestions for improvement, video models (Bandura and Walters, 1963), written materials, and supervisor's comments. Operant techniques (Skinner, 1953) are stressed, in that appropriate interviewer behavior is rewarded; the emphasis is on positive growth and relatively little attention is paid to interviewer errors. The positive approach of operant psychology coupled with specific suggestions is important in rapid trainee growth.

However, microcounseling training also involves important *relationship skills* on the part of the supervisor. It is possible for a routine to develop in which the teacher of skills loses personal involvement with the trainee. When this happens, the trainee may still learn the skills but appears to have trouble generalizing them to actual interviewing settings. Therefore, a friendly, warm and genuine attitude on the part of the individual supervising a microtraining session is essential. *Most important, the supervisor in a microcounseling training session must model the skills he is teaching.* If the supervisor does not attend to the trainee when teaching attending behavior or note appropriate emotions and feelings when teaching reflection of feeling, little learning in the situation will occur. Rogers (1957) might term this supervisory behavior as genuiness or congruence. Regardless of whether one favors the precision of learning theory or the warmth of phenomenology, it seems essential for successful microcounseling training that the supervisor be congruent with his trainee and model what he teaches.

Many alternatives and additions to this basic framework are possible. Perhaps most important among them is the recycling of the entire process; here, the trainee at step nine simply repeats steps three through eight, thus obtaining extra practice and reinforcement of the skill in question. The nine-step training process, including two five-minute interviews, takes approximately one hour; recycling the process brings training to a two-hour period, a time which seems to be maximum for participation. If the skill is not learned at this point, trainees are asked to return for further sessions.

It is possible to vary styles of supervision, to use multiple supervisors, or even to eliminate the supervisor. A programmed text has been successfully used in place of the written manual in some studies. The extent of video feedback and the number of models shown to the trainee can be varied. In some cases, role playing and rehearsal of the specific skill to be demonstrated have been utilized as an additional step before the trainee returns for another counseling session.

With some trainees, it is possible to teach more than one skill at a time. With others, it is desirable to break a skill into even smaller component parts before the central skill is practiced. For example, some interviewers may need to learn how to maintain eye contact before they can attempt general listening skills. Considerable variation has been observed in the skills individuals bring to microtraining sessions. However, with apt supervision, careful selection of skills leading to more complex behaviors, and ample practice, we believe that virtually every person can significantly improve their interviewing skills.

While alternative microtraining models are possible, we have found that the basic nine-step model described above or a recycling of three sessions seems most successful. The multidimensional learning procedures of experiential, cognitive, and observational learning combined with self-observation make an impactful training package.

Microcounseling is based on several essential propositions. First, it is possible to lessen the complexity of the counseling or interviewing process through *focusing on single skills.* The goal of the trainee is to master one skill at a time rather than demonstrating competence in all areas simultaneously. This provides the student with an opportunity to see himself improve immediately in one area, which helps him develop more difficult skills at later training stages.

Second, microtraining techniques provide important opportunities for *self-observation and confrontation.* Immediately after engaging in a counseling session, the trainee and the supervisor have the opportunity to view the trainee's behavior and the client's reactions. Provision of instantaneous feedback serves as a guideline to future interview performance.

Third, interviewers can learn from *observing video models* demonstrating the skills they are seeking to learn. Each specific skill is demonstrated on videotape by a skilled counselor. Not only does the trainee hear what good techniques in counseling are but he sees them in action.

Fourth, microcounseling is a method which *can be used to teach interviewing skills in a wide area of diverse theoretical and practical frameworks.* Psychoanalytic interpretation skills, Rogerian reflection of feeling, interpretation of vocational tests, and asking questions in an employment interview can all be taught within a microtraining framework.

Fifth, microtraining sessions are *real interviewing.* While role-played or simulated counseling sessions are sometimes used in this method, the trainee soon finds himself assuming a real counseling role. Frequently the volunteer client finds himself discussing actual problems. A common finding is that clients appear to appreciate the opportunity to have someone listen to them and volunteer to return for more sessions of this type.

THE USES OF MICROTRAINING

Microcounseling is designed to bridge the gap between theory and practice, between classroom and interview session, between what is said and what is done. Following are some settings in which microcounseling has demonstrated its usefulness.

Safe Practice in Counseling and Interviewing Skills

Many are concerned about "unleashing" the beginning thera-pist on the first client. The casual observer of a novice clinician often wonders if the wrong person is doing the interviewing. Full of anxieties, trying to remember a list of do's and don'ts, the beginning interviewer is often most ineffective. While not all interviewers or therapists go through this experience, most would admit that awkward early sessions happen all too often.

As a result of this confusion, clients are lost and sometimes never return to another therapist. Good candidates for a job are missed; a student may end up in the wrong college. If the counseling profession is capable of helping clients, it is also capable of damaging them.

Similarly, interviewers may be injured by their first session or sessions. A cycle of self-doubt and self-blame may be gener-

committed to this type of approach. Microcounseling forces one
to identfiy what he is doing.

Thus, microcounseling skills in this book are presented in
terms which are definable and replicable in many situations.
The application of any one skill is not counseling or interviewing;
it is practice in a specific skill. Counseling and interviewing exist
at a higher level, in which the individual has many skills and
uses them appropriately in response to the interviewing situation
in which he finds himself. The skilled counselor or interviewer
does not necessarily think of the skills he uses.

The concept of *tacit knowing* as used by Polanyi may help
show the relationship between the specific experiential skills of
microcounseling and the skilled counselor who has many skills
available to him. When one swings a golf club well, sings a
song beautifully, or responds appropriately to a client, there is
tacit knowledge of what one has done. Moreover, if the golfer,
singer, or interviewer thought in detail of all the actions or
specific behaviors he engaged in, the quality of the action would
not be possible. Many specific behaviors have been integrated
into one large, natural action. Some learn these actions more
easily than others. Some counselors learn to attend or listen
almost immediately. Others need to learn that eye contact,
physical relaxation, and verbal following are three behaviors
important in listening. As they practice these behaviors, they
become integrated into a large whole and no longer need to
be stressed, as they have become part of the person.

At higher levels, the counselor who has many skills can draw
on them readily and naturally. He has had sufficient practice
and experience so that these skills have become part of him.
One of the major objectives of the microtraining framework is to
identify a wide variety of skills useful in interviewing and then
allow the trainee to practice experientially and finally make them
a part of himself, drawing on them as he feels the need.

Finally, it must be recognized that there is more than one
alternative route to excellence in golf, singing, or interviewing.
Some come by these skills naturally; their life experience seems
to be such that they need not think about what they are doing.
Even they, however, often have to go back and practice details

before they can integrate difficult concepts or problems into their behavior (e.g. the golfer practicing putting if he is "off," the singer rehearsing a difficult passage, the therapist reflecting on what went wrong in the last session). Many people do not come by complex skills of living naturally and easily. Microtraining is proposed as one method through which they can develop skills which otherwise might not be possible.

A Research Tool

The microtraining framework provides a useful laboratory for interviewing research. A major problem in counseling research is the isolation of the many variables involved in the counselor-client interaction. When viewed over a fifty-minute session, the complexity of the interview becomes almost overwhelming. Variables in the interviewing process can be sorted out more easily in the microtraining framework, thus allowing the researcher to investigate his specific area of interest more closely. Control of verbal comments or nonverbal communication by the counselor is more easily obtained. Variables such as length of session, varieties of training techniques, client problems, and a host of other variables can be more easily manipulated.

Microtraining offers a framework for a host of controlled studies in counselor training and counseling itself. What are the important dimensions of learning in microcounseling? Is it supervision? Is it feedback? Is it viewing the models? Or is it perhaps the interaction of these factors with a particular trainee? What interviewing skills seem to help which client at what time? The short-term sessions provide an excellent laboratory for the study of mutual reinforcement patterns of counselor and client. These and other research possibilities will be considered in more detail at a later point.

The microcounseling framework provides an opportunity to test laboratory research in a more applied setting before direct translation to operational practice is made. Various problems of applying research to practice can be studied and resolved in the more controlled and standard situation provided by microcounseling.

SUMMARY

This chapter has identified microcounseling as a structural innovation which may be applied in a variety of situations with a multitude of content dimensions. The structures and methods of these techniques may be used in counselor or interviewer training, client pretraining, helping a retarded individual prepare for a job interview, as a supplement to marriage counseling, or any of a wide variety of training situations.

The focus on specific skills as opposed to the totality of the interview allows one to approach the interview more analytically and to develop a more sophisticated understanding of one's own skills and limitations. Microtraining is useful for research and as a framework for in-service or preservice counselor training.

The multidimensional training approach of microcounseling utilizes several aspects of learning theory, the most important of which is experiential. The trainee has the opportunity to practice and demonstrate that he has learned the skill in question. In addition, he has the opportunity to look at himself in comparison to expert counselors. While the basic microcounseling model as outlined has many alternatives, evidence suggests that the multimedia, multifaceted approach of the basic model is most effective.

It is important to note that structural innovations are highly subject to value decisions made by the individual using the approach. It is conceivable that one could use a microcounseling framework to teach counselors skills which are irrelevant or even damaging to the client. While this may be unlikely, the possibility of using this method in unwise ways must be considered. Further, it is not a panacea which will make everyone a skilled interviewer. It should, however, be a useful tool to help interviewers become more effective.

Chapter Two

MICROCOUNSELING IN PERSPECTIVE

John R. Moreland

INSTRUCTION IN BASIC psychotherapeutic and interviewing skills is carried out in educational institutions with students preparing for widely varying professions. The personnel executive, the psychotherapist, and the school counselor all require interviewing training. Further, due to the constantly increasing demand for mental health workers, more and more "lay therapists," "indigenous helpers," and other subprofessionals are being trained each year for therapeutic roles formerly occupied exclusively by professional therapists. Unfortunatley, this instruction has often been of a hit-or-miss apprentice type, with intuition or clinical art stressed over precise and defined behaviors, and trial-and-error learning over systematic teaching. In a rather uncomfortable analogy, Christine McQuire (in Wolberg, 1967) compared a psychotherapy supervisor to a football coach who sends his team out to play, several games after which they report to him how they have done and what they intend to do in the next few games. Fortunately for the sport of football, such coaches would not be around long. However, in psychotherapeutic and interviewing training, such procedures are frequently the rule rather than the exception.

More than ten years ago, Rogers (1957, p. 76) decried the state of training procedures in psychotherapy when he made the following comment:

> Considering the fact that one-third of present-day psychologists have a special interest in the field of psychotherapy, we would expect that a great deal of attention might be given to the problem of training individuals to engage in the therapeutic process. . . . For the most part, this field is characterized by a rarity of research and a plentitude of platitudes.

15

The situation today is little better than it was then. Matarazzo, Wiens, and Saslow (1966, p. 608), after an extensive review of the literature, concluded the following:

> From the studies cited and from our review of the literature, we have concluded that there is essentially no published research regarding the teaching of psychotherapy, the supervisory process, how learning of effective psychotherapy takes place, and how to teach psychotherapy efficiently. Many reports of training programs are available and it is evident that many psychotherapists talk about teaching, but few report systematic innovations, comparison of methods, and/or student skill before and after a course of instruction.

More recently, Whitely (1969), after reviewing the counselor-education literature, reached much the same conclusion.

A number of factors are responsible for this paucity of research. First, psychotherapy itself has been viewed as a private interaction between therapist and patient, removed from any form of public scrutiny, and the supervisory process has been seen in the same light. Second, because until recently, researchers and other observers have been excluded from the therapist's inner office, relatively little is known about what actually occurs in the therapeutic process. This has made it exceedingly difficult to reach any agreement on what student-therapists should learn in supervision. As a result, various schools of training have tended to view the acquisition of conceptual-strategical skills and the resolution of the trainee's counter-transference feelings as the proper content of the supervisory process. However, Matarazzo, Wiens, and Saslow (1966) have reviewed ways in which the acquisition of knowledge might be facilitated by opening up to observation the supervisory process and the student therapist's training experiences.

It is our contention that traditional therapeutic training has neglected explicitly teaching students about the nature of the interviewing process. Recent studies in microcounseling have demonstrated that there are specific behavioral skills which an interviewer can utilize to facilitate a client's self-exploration. These skills, serving as a bridge between the trainee's classroom learning and his applied training experiences, may actually facilitate the type of learning which traditional training procedures have emphasized.

In the past, training programs appear to have assumed that the worst that can happen to the trainee's patient is that he fails to improve. Students' patients could improve or stay at the same level of functioning, but they were not expected to deteriorate as a result of being seen by a trainee. However, Patterson (1968) has recently pointed out that this assumption is pure fantasy. Counseling, even when practiced by experienced counselors or therapists, may lead to client deterioration (Truax, 1961; Truax and Carkhuff, 1967; and Truax and Wargo, 1966). In addition, Strupp's (1970) data suggest that a patient's reactions to the initial stages of therapy are crucial in determining its outcome. Therefore, it appears desirable to help a student make the transition from the classroom to the therapy session as smoothly as possible. Before beginning a discussion of facilitative-behavioral skills, it seems beneficial to review various existing models of therapeutic training, thereby placing microcounseling in a broader perspective.

TRAINING PROGRAMS IN PSYCHOTHERAPEUTIC SKILLS

In this section, several traditional counselor and therapist training models will be discussed and their potential weaknesses reviewed. Microcounseling will be discussed within this framework, not as a substitute for any of these training models but as a supplement to them. Microcounseling is a technique which can help student counselors, regardless of theoretical orientation, experience a smooth transition from their classroom to their initial practicum or internship activities.

Psychoanalytic Model

Students trained under this model are expected to possess a highly developed and refined conceptual grasp of psychoanalytic theory. Only after a student has read widely and attended innumerable lectures and seminars on psychoanalysis and psychoanalytic psychotherapy is he assigned his first control patient. Using Ekstein and Wallerstein's (1958) model of supervision, the trainee's self-report of what occurred between himself and the patient serves as the sole data upon which the student's learning within the supervisory process is based. As Reivich and Geertsma (1969) point out, proponents of this model rely exclusively upon this process orientation to supervision because they stress the importance of the student's conscious or unconscious tendencies to distort what actually occurred in therapy. In essence, the trainee's supervised experiences are of a therapeutic nature, as they aim to help the student work through difficulties in describing sessions with his patients spontaneously, clearly, and cogently.

During analytic training, the student is expected to expand and refine his conceptual-strategical skills and to recognize and resolve countertransference feelings elicited by his patient. To accomplish these goals, the trainee must first work through transference feelings toward his supervisor (problems about learning) which inhibit his mastery of the learning problems. The learning products of this model appear to be primarily internal, conceptual entities which somehow are reflected in the trainee's actual therapy behavior. The mechanisms producing this transformation or the behavioral end-products have not been stated explicitly. At no point in this process is there an attempt to observe or modify the student-therapist's actual behavior with the patient, despite the fact that the leap from reading about psychotherapy to conducting psychotherapy is large and awkward.

Rogerian Client-Centered Training

Just as Rogers' theory of personality and personality change was revolutionary when compared with the psychoanalytic models which preceded it, the modifications he recommended in the training of future therapists were equally daring. Rogers suggested opening both therapeutic and supervisory relationships to public observation. Rogerians were first to decry the lack of objective data about what occurs in psychotherapy and to note the absence of evaluations of training techniques for student-therapists.

In an attempt to make training procedures more systematic and amenable to assessment, Rogers (1957) presented what was at that time the most explicitly formulated suggestions for teaching psychotherapy techniques to novices. He suggested that initially students listen to recording of experienced and inexperienced therapists doing live therapy. In this way, they could learn to discriminate between good and bad techniques. The next step had both vicarious and experiential components. He suggested that students obtain a direct acquaintance with psychotherapy by observing a series of interviews conducted by experienced therapists participating in group therapy and/or undergoing individual therapy. During the final stage of training, Rogers suggested that the trainee be allowed to actually carry on psychotherapy under the direct supervision of an experienced therapist. He also recommended that teaching devices such as tape recorded interviews and multiple-therapist cases be utilized as beneficial learning vehicles for the novice.

The first two steps in Rogers' training program can be viewed as one of the first attempts to establish a formal training bridge between what the novice has learned in the classroom and what he is supposed to do in actual therapy or interview situations. He was the first to present a means for helping novices acquire facilitative interview behaviors.

Whether or not Rogers' innovations accomplish their goal is questionable. While the first two steps of this training model are designed to provide novice interviewers with ample vicarious opportunities to acquire counseling skills, specific behaviors which are to be discriminated and internalized are not identified. For example, if a student-interviewer listens to a therapy tape or observes a live lession and then discriminates whether it was a good or a bad session, it does not mean that he has successfully discriminated what the therapist did or did not do to make it a successful or unsuccessful session.

Didactic-Experiential Training

Truax and Carkhuff (1967) have developed a training program which still reflects a Rogerian influence but represents a substantial departure from the model outlined above. They selected as training goals therapists qualities which differentiated successful from unsuccessful therapists in the Wisconsin Schizophrenia Project (Rogers, *et al.* 1967). A substantial number of studies coming from this project demonstrated that patients of therapists who were rated high on warmth, empathy, and genuineness had positive therapeutic outcomes, while patients whose counselors were rated low on these dimensions either did not improve or deteriorated (Truax, 1961; Truax and Carkhuff, 1967; Truax, Carkhuff and Kodman, 1965).

Truax and Carkhuff, assuming that warmth, empathy and genuineness are both the necessary and sufficient conditions for therapeutic change, outlined a training program which emphasized the development of these therapist characteristics. They suggested that initially, new students listen to selected positive and negative audiotape samples of therapists rated high on the necessary qualities doing actual therapy. After the students have learned what constitutes high and low warmth, empathy, and genuineness, they should be taught to further discriminate these qualities by learning to rate the tapes they are listening to on seven- or nine-point scales.

The assumption of the Truax-Carkhuff program is that if students can learn to recognize the presence or absence of these qualities in other therapists, they will automatically incorporate these qualities into their own interview behavior. Because they assume that all therapists should have insight into their behavior and its impact on others, Truax and Carkhuff suggest that all student-therapists should have a group-therapy experience. In addition, once the trainee has actually begun doing therapy himself, the supervisor should relate to the student in a highly warm, empathic, and genuine manner. In this way, the supervisor not only provides the trainee with an appropriate role-model, but establishes the conditions under which the novice can most easily engage in self-exploration. This model is similar to the previous two in its emphasis on establishing means for the trainees learning to deal with feelings and conflicts elicited by their training experiences. However, Truax and Carkhuff have emphasized more than Rogers the acquisition of specifiable facilitative interviewer skills prior to the trainee's involvement in actual counseling situations.

While Truax and Carkhuff have succeeded in developing a training program aimed at helping students acquire certain specifiable skills which previous research has shown are correlated with therapeutic change, they failed in their early work to define explicitly what behaviors constitute empathic, warm, or genuine behavior.

More recently, Carkhuff (1969a, 1969b) has refined and elaborated the training model initially presented by him and Truax. He has operationalized empathic understanding, incorporated warmth into the dimension of respect and extended the therapeutic equation to include counselor initiative dimensions of confrontation and immediacy. In addition, he has added systematic programs for the development of effective courses of action for the client. In this work, Carkhuff presents an elaborate conceptual schema for counselor training, based upon many studies related to these methods. Carkhuff's most significant contribution may be his emphasis on evaluating the results of counselor training programs and then modifying or changing training programs so as to produce more effective counselors. Also, the concept of facilitative conditions developed by Carkhuff is increasingly recognized as central to the helping professions.

Recent Training Innovations

Microcounseling has been presented as a training device which can be an important supplement to existing training models. During the past several years, other interview-training techniques have evolved which also effectively supplement professional counselor and therapist training programs. In addition, these innovations have served as stimuli for the formulation of microcounseling as presently conceived and for this reason deserve mention at this point.

Reivich and Geertsma (1969) reviewed the literature dealing with the use of observational media in the training of student therapists. They describe a training model based on the use of videotape and incorporating such features as videotaped demonstrations of desired behaviors, self-observation by the novice, and utilizing videotapes of the novice as the focal point of the supervisory session. This model was not meant to replace the traditional emphasis on assisting students to acquire conceptual-strategical skills but to facilitate and elaborate on this important area. They feel that by utilizing observational media, the trainees will be better able to translate behavioral events into theoretical concepts and conceptions of therapists activities into behavioral events. Kagan and Krathwohl (1967) have also discussed the use of videotape to help novice interviewers learn to counsel by observing their own sessions. More recently, Kagan (1969) has utilized this method to teach medical students how to interview patients while gathering important information such as the medical history.

Implicit in the work of Reivich and Geertsma and that of Kagan and his associates is the assumption that by utilizing videotapes of the novice's counseling sessions, the trainee and his supervisor can identify and strengthen positive facilitative behaviors and change nonfacilitative behaviors. However, Whitely (1969) and others have pointed out that currently we are unable to adequately define what constitutes effective counseling behavior. Reivich and Geertsma confronted this issue and suggested that the use of videotape may serve to facilitate the study of both criterion performance and the process of learning to be a psychotherapist.

Microcounseling, with its emphasis on the teaching of positive facilitative behaviors, appears to maximize the use of videotape as both a teaching and a research instrument. Before model tapes of discrete interviewer skills can be formulated, individual skills must be well operationalized so that they can be easily discriminated by and communicated to the trainee. All the microcounseling skills developed to date have been empirically related to either verifiable outcome criteria or to changes in counselee behavior which are in turn related to outcome criteria. In addition, the microcounseling paradigm lends itself to the study of the trainee's learning process and to relating changes in interview behavior to events within the supervisory or microcounseling paradigm.

Evaluations of Present Training Programs

Having reviewed major programs for training in basic psychotherapeutic skills, it is now appropriate to ask whether or not these programs are effective. Studies evaluating current training practices are few and far between. Whitely (1969, p. 35) while reviewing the literature dealing with the effectiveness of existing counselor-education programs made the following conclusion:

> Despite the importance of this topic and its centrality to the profession, very little was available in the literature. Published work was of generally low quality, superficial, and so narrowly defined as to be misleading in the implications which might be drawn from it. Regrettably, evaluation as currently (practiced) does not appear to be a term with any substance in counselor education programs.

Carkhuff (1969a, 1969b) has reviewed the literature evaluating the effectiveness of trained lay personnel in conducting counseling sessions with live clients. This increasingly impressive body of literature demonstrates that several types of patients or clients can be helped by lay persons trained in a variety of ways (Appleby, 1963; Carkhuff and Truax, 1965; Magoon and Golann, 1966; Mendel and Rapport, 1963; Poser, 1966; and Rioch *et al.*, 1963). After reviewing the literature comparing the effectiveness of lay counselors with professionally trained counselors, Carkhuff (1969a, p. 7) concludes that "While the number of comparable studies is limited, with both outpatients and inpatients lay persons effect changes on the indexes assessed that are at least as great or, all too frequently, greater (never significantly less), than professionals." Carkhuff attributes this surprising comparison to the fact that the goals of professional training are multiple, with primary emphasis on the development of discriminative, as opposed to communicative abilities. Most lay programs, on the other hand, emphasize the acquisition of interviewer skills which communicate the conditions facilitative of the clients' self-exploration.

A number of interesting and highly revealing studies have evaluated the effectiveness of current professional programs. Among other things, these studies point out the need to incorporate techniques for helping students acquire facilitative-behavioral interviewer skills in traditional training programs. Bergin and Solomon (1969) evaluated the level of accurate empathy in tape-recorded therapy sessions. They examined eighteen postinternship students from clinical psychology pro-

grams approved by the American Psychological Association
(APA). The best of these students received only intermediate
ratings on this measure. Perhaps their most interesting finding
was that the students' level of accurate empathy correlated
−.17 with their previous practicum grades and −.16 with their
academic grades. Mellon (in Truax and Carkhuff, 1967) assessed
the level of accurate empathy in tape-recorded sessions of
twenty-eight postpracticum counselor trainees in APA-approved
counseling psychology programs. He reported a correlation of
−.008 between the students' level of accurate empathy and
grades for their practicum performance. If one accepts the
assumption that accurate empathy is an important therapist
quality, then these two studies suggest that current training
programs in clinical and counseling psychology reward students
on the basis of factors which are irrelevant to their ability to
function therapeutically.

   Carkhuff, Kratochvil, and Friel (1968) had clinical and nonclinical first- and fourth-year graduate students in psychology
perform forty-five-minute interviews which were then rated for
the level of the interviewers' warmth, empathy, and genuineness.
They found that first-year clinical students functioned at a higher
level on all three of the measures than first year nonclinical
students. However, this difference "washed out" by the fourth
year. Recognizing the difficulties of interpreting crossectional
data, these investigators had clinical graduate students at a
different school perform forty-five-minute interviews at the
beginning of their first year and again at the end of their second
year. After rating these interviews on the three measures—
accurate empathy, respect, and genuineness—they found that by
the end of their second year, the clinical students had deteriorated in their functioning levels of these three qualities.

   These two studies suggest that not only are two APA-approved
graduate training programs in clinical psychology unable to assist
students to develop certain psychotherapeutic skills considered
essential by virtually all schools of psychotherapy but they are
also unable to help the students maintain their initial levels of
functioning on these measures. Carkhuff, Kratochvil and Friel
examined one possible explanation for this deficiency in graduate

training. They evaluated the functioning level of nine professors of clinical psychology at one of the universities on each of the three measures. They found that their level of functioning was well below average. Anthony and Carkhuff (1970), in an evaluation of a rehabilitation counseling program, found that the trainees acquired only those skills which were explicitly emphasized by the counselors in charge of the training program. Given that the faculty of professional training programs communicate only low levels of those therapist qualities which appear related to important outcome criteria, it is not surprising that professional training programs appear to have so little success in producing students who can communicate high levels of these conditions.

The studies summarized here suggest that current professional training programs emphasize the development of conceptual abilities and the mastery of content areas, to the exclusion of helping students acquire behaviors which can facilitate self-exploration on the patient's part and effect therapeutic change. In the next section, we will look at actual novice interviewer behavior and its impact on interviewees. From such a review, we can begin to define positive facilitative interviewer behaviors which can be taught to novice interviewers.

STUDIES OF NOVICE INTERVIEWER BEHAVIOR

Unfortunately, most studies which have attempted to assess the nature of the novice interviewer's behavior have relied almost exclusively on the novice's ability to recall retrospectively what his interaction with the patient was like. Porter (1950, in Matarazzo, Wiens, and Saslow, 1966) reported developing a questionnaire which he used to assess modifications in beginning counselors' attitudes by collecting pretraining and posttraining questionnaire data. Heine, Aldrich, Draper, Meuser, Tippett, and Trosman (1962) attempted to evaluate the effectiveness of a program for teaching psychotherapy to fourth year medical students and assessed the students' learning through their responses on a self-report questionnaire.

The utilization of retrospective self-report data in formulating

an idea of a novice's actual interview behavior can lead to a
distorted, inaccurate picture of what the novice actually does
with a patient. Blocksma and Porter (1947), in a now-classic
study, presented the results of their evaluation of an interview-
skills training program conducted at the University of Chicago
Counseling Center. They obtained both questionnaire and observational data from actual interviews conducted by the trainees.
In a pretraining questionnaire, students reported that they would
respond 89 percent of the time by reflecting the feeling of the
client. However, only 11 percent of the trainees' responses in
the live interview were reflective in nature. There appears to
have been little relationship between what the students reported
they would do and what they actually did in the interview. In
addition, there was no relationship between a trainee's posttraining questionnaire responses and his supervisors' ratings of
his skill one year later. However, there was such a relationship
between the trainee's actual use of client-centered techniques in
the posttraining interview and his subsequent on-the-job performance. The Blocksma and Porter study suggests the importance of obtaining actual observational measures of the interviewers' behaviors rather than relying on the interviewers' reports
of their behavior.

Phillips and Matarazzo (1962) analyzed the content of
novice interviewers' interview behavior before and after training.
After pretraining measures were obtained, the six students in
Group A were assigned two therapy cases whom they saw once
a week for ten weeks. During supervision, the students reported
their interviews to their supervisors, and on the basis of their
reports received conceptual and technical suggestions. The four
students in Group B were observed by their supervisor as they
performed an interview once a week. Following each observation,
the supervisor and the student would discuss the student's actual
interview behavior, and the supervisor would make recommenda-
tions for specific behavioral changes. Group B students, in
addition to increasing in their use of nondirective, communication-
facilitating techniques, became more active and influence-
oriented during their interviews than did Group A students.
It is of interest that those students whose training was primarily

behavioral in substance developed interviewer behaviors which more closely resemble the behaviors of Strupp's (1960) experienced therapists.

Matarazzo, Phillips, Wiens, and Saslow (1965) attempted to measure actual novice behaviors and to relate changes in these behavior patterns to the students' training. The trainees were six second-year medical students who had just completed a six-month introductory course in psychiatry which included lectures and demonstrations of general interviewing methods. Trainees conducted thirty-five-minute interviews with each of six patients before they began a summer clerkship in psychiatry. After pretraining data were obtained, each trainee was assigned two newly admitted psychiatric patients whom he saw for eight weeks in intensive individual psychotherapy. Each student received traditional supervision as described above.

At the end of the summer clerkship, every trainee again interviewed the six patients he had interviewed during the pretraining data collection. The pretraining and the posttraining interviews were then analyzed behaviorally, using the Chapple Interaction Chronograph (Matarazzo, Saslow, and Matarazzo, 1956), and qualitatively, using the Checklist of Therapist "Errors" Behavior which was formulated by the authors. Each therapist utterance was rated as good, fair, or poor. Each response that was classified as either fair or poor was then categorized in terms of the type of error it represented. The check list contained three main types of errors—errors of focus, faulty role definition, and faulty facilitation of communication.

The investigators found that there was a significant decrease in errors in all the categories from the pretraining to the posttraining interviews. In the pretraining interviews, most of the errors were in the faulty facilitation of communication category, while in the posttraining interview, the most frequent errors were in the errors-of-focus category. For example, during pretraining interviews, the student-therapists frequently interrupted the patients, asked closed questions and made long, awkward speeches. During posttraining interviews, the interviewers were more inclined to focus on irrelevant aspects of significant material or to make noncontributory statements or to ask questions which neither aided nor impeded the progress of the interview. The trainees appeared to have learned from their experience to get a patient to talk, although they were still not too clear about what he should be discussing. By using the Chapple Interaction Chronograph data, the investigators discovered that the greater the number of errors made by the student-therapists, the shorter was the patient's average utterance and the smaller the percent of the patient's actual talk time. When the trainee's errors were minimized, both the patient's average utterance time and the patient's percentage of talk time increased significantly. The authors concluded that ". . . the students had learned a few simple rules about what not to do but they had substituted some other poor behaviors, and still did not know what to listen for or what to do in regard to responding sensitively to significant cues" (p. 52).

This study is important because it was among the first to actually utilize pretraining and posttraining behavioral measures in the evaluation of a psychotherapy training program. However, the authors' conclusions indicate that while trainees learned not to do certain things, they had been unable to acquire more appropriate behaviors. This strongly suggests the possibility that a more behavioral approach to training in psychotherapeutic skills, where specific interview behaviors are taught, could be beneficially integrated as a central part of the student's early training experiences.

Matarazzo, Wiens, and Saslow (1966) reported a more thorough analysis of the Interaction Chronograph data which was used in the Matarazzo, Phillips, Wiens, and Saslow (1965) study. They found that the behavior of each patient was little affected by differences among students. However, the frequency and duration of the trainees' interview behavior in the pretraining interviews was determined largely by the patient they were interviewing. The authors interpreted this as an indication that the students had not yet developed a stable interviewing style. During the posttraining interviews, the students had established a more stable, individual style.

Cartwright (1968), in her article in the *Annual Review of Psychology*, offered a positive reaction to this work and suggested that more training programs and techniques should be developed which attempt to ascertain types of interviewer errors and consequently orient the trainee's experiences toward the elimination of these undesirable behaviors. Ultimately, as Cartwright has reminded us, the goal of research must be to connect studies of effective instruction to specified clinician behaviors; these, in turn, should be associated with specified client behavioral changes both within treatment and, more importantly, outside of and after treatment. Short of this very large endeavor, it is possible to identify clinician behaviors whose immediately facilitative effects have some empirical support, to define these concretely, and to attempt to teach them directly.

A number of conclusions can be reached about novice-interviewer behavior. In general, beginning interviewers do not possess a stable repertoire of behaviors or techniques, and their behavior is largely determined by the patient they happen to be interviewing. Beginning interviewers spend too much time talking, interrupt the patient, ask closed-ended questions; make long, awkward speeches; and lapse into long, unplanned silences.

Following their initial training experiences, beginning counselors spend less time talking, interrupt the patient less, ask more open-ended questions, make fewer irrelevant comments, ask for more specific examples, and inquire why patients behaved and felt as they did. They also use paraphrases and feeling reflections as perception checks, communication facilitators, and techniques for emphasizing recurrent patterns and themes. These more active, newly acquired behaviors were more prevalent among students who were trained by supervisors who utilized a concrete behavioral analysis of the trainee's interview behavior during supervision.

While these studies illustrate the possibility of isolating, defining, and teaching concrete behaviors which are basic to a novice's acquisition of clinical interviewing skills and the advantages of fitting such instruction into the natural stages in the acquisition process, they have some problems as an instructional approach. Some aspects of the beginner's behavior were unchanged (e.g. faulty role definition) and others ignored (especially nonverbal affective and motor behaviors). No model of good interview behaviors was available to the students. Feedback to the students was delayed and relatively abstract, often being in the form of frequency counts of each error with perhaps a few examples recalled or transcribed, assuming that the supervisor had observed the interview session.

Microcounseling

An approach to instruction in basic clinical skills which overcomes these defects is that of microcounseling, first reported by Ivey, Normington, Miller, Morrill, and Haase (1968). This instructional technique has the advantage of dividing interviewer behavior into small units and making possible direct feedback to the trainee, thus facilitating behavior change. At this point, it should be stated explicitly that we view interviewing as more complex than merely emitting discrete, canned, or mechanical behaviors at the appropriate moment. Microcounseling simply provides the vehicle for the student to acquire necessary, discrete skills which, once delineated and acquired, can be internalized and spontaneously emitted. Microcounseling is based on the assumption that interviewer behavior is extremely complex and can best be taught by breaking it down into discrete behavioral units until the trainee has so internalized each individual skill that it can be emitted spontaneously and without premeditation.

Ivey, Normington, Miller, Morrill, and Haase (1968) first utilized the microcounseling technique to teach three different groups of beginning counselors one of the following three interviewer skills: attending behavior, reflection of feeling, or summarization of feeling. Ivey *et al.* defined attending behavior in terms of three highly reliable, easily identifiable component behaviors—eye contact, relaxed postural position with appropriate gestures, and accurate verbal following behavior. Accurate reflection of feeling was seen as a focused aspect of attending behavior in which the interviewer selectively attended to the feeling component of the client's communication and then reflected empathic understanding back to him. Summarization was very similar to reflection, except that it covered a longer temporal period and was more integrative than was reflection of feeling.

Using microcounseling training in one- and two-hour training periods, Ivey *et al.* found that beginning prepracticum counseling students showed significant changes in attending behavior, reflection of feeling, and summarization of feeling.

Ivey *et al.* obtained the clients' reactions to both the premicrocounseling and the postmicrocounseling interviewers by requiring them to complete the Counselor Effectiveness Scale (Ivey, Miller, Morrill, and Normington, 1967) and a relationship questionnaire adapted from Truax and Carkhuff (1967). The validity of the specific skills taught via the microcounseling paradigm is attested to by the fact that every pretraining and posttraining comparison of the clients' reactions was positive and significant. Not only were they able to define in concrete terms the interview skills of attending behavior, reflection of feeling and summarization of feeling but they also demonstrated that these skills could be taught to novice interviewers within the microcounseling paradigm. In addition, by demonstrating that the client's reactions to the student interviewer were significantly more positive once the student acquired the specified skills, Ivey *et al.* successfully met Cartwright's (1968) reminder that the goal of training research must be to connect studies of effective instruction to specified client behavioral changes.

While the Ivey *et al.* study was the first to demonstrate the efficacy of microcounseling training both as an instructional medium for the acquisition of basic psychotherapeutic skills and as a research paradigm, there have been a number of more recent studies which deserve mention, as they have contributed to the validity of the instructional method. Moreland, Phillips, Ivey, and Lockhart (1970) have utilized microcounseling to teach six interviewer skills to first-year clinical psychology graduate students. The skills were attending behavior, minimal activity, openended questions, reflection of feeling, paraphrase, and summarization. This study was the first to demonstrate that the effects of microcounseling training generalized from the instructional lab to actual interview situations with real-life patients. Haase and DiMattia (1970) have demonstrated that the skills of attending behavior, reflection of feeling, and expression of feeling can be taught to previously untrained counseling support personnel by utilizing the microcounseling paradigm. Further, they found (Haase, DiMattia, and Guttman, 1970) that these skills maintained themselves over a year's time.

The preceding studies have been concerned with training counselors in basic interview skills which are applicable to many different types of interview situations. Miller, Morrill, Ivey, Normington, and Uhlemann (1969) have demonstrated that the microcounseling skill of selective attending can be used to shape a client's verbal behavior toward talking about his attitudes about tests. Related to this study, Miller, Morrill, and Uhlemann (1970) have successfully used microcounseling to teach counseling students certain broad skills which are specific to conveying interpretations of psychological test data to clients.

In an important variation, Higgins, Ivey, and Uhlemann (1970) have used the microcounseling paradigm to teach college students the interpersonal skills of direct, mutual communication, skills which are closely related to those emphasized in encounter groups. In this article, they raised the possibility that microcounseling could be used to train clients in therapy to use more effective interpersonal skills in their everyday, extratherapeutic interpersonal relationships. Donk (1969) found it possible to teach hospitalized mental patients the skill of attending behavior, and this new interpersonal skill generalized to the patients' ward behavior. In a related study, Haase, Forsyth, Julius, and Lee (1969) showed that clients at a university counseling center, trained in the skill of expression of feeling prior to being seen by a counselor, expressed more feeling in their initial counseling session than did clients who did not receive such training.

As can be seen from this brief description of the studies which have appeared since the first microcounseling study, there is developing an ever-increasing list of isolated, concrete, behaviorally defined interviewer skills which can be taught within the microcounseling framework. The work of Moreland, Phillips, Ivey, and Lockhart has demonstrated the feasibility of defining these skills to the degree that good and bad models can be made for an increasingly large variety of interviewer behaviors. In addition, from a training point of view, these studies have shown that a variety of skills can be taught to trainees with minimal feedback delay, thus maximizing learning.

SUMMARY

A model for counselor training was presented in the early part of this chapter, which conceptualized effective training programs as leading to skill acquisition in three broad, mutually exclusive areas. A novice counselor should receive help in developing facilitative-behavioral interviewer skills and conceptual-strategical skills and also should be provided with opportunities to resolve and to learn to deal with feelings elicited by contact with clients. The psychoanalytic model of training addresses itself almost exclusively to the development of conceptual strategical skills and the resolution of countertransference feelings. The client-centered and didactic-experiential models have recognized the importance of helping novices acquire facilitative-behavioral interviewer skills. Both of these training conceptualizations suffer from their inability to isolate and specify discrete objective interviewer behaviors which the novice can be taught and the acquisition of which lead to predictable changes in client behavior, either outside of the counseling situation or within a counseling session.

Studies of novice interviewer behavior have revealed that beginning counselors make a variety of easily identifiable errors. These mistakes suggest equally identifiable and teachable positive counselor behaviors which can be taught to the novices prior to their initial real-life interview experiences in order to help them be more effective in their first applied encounters. Microcounseling, with its emphasis on systematically teaching students positive facilitative interviewer behaviors rather than relying on the students to acquire these skills in a trial-and-error fashion, is seen as an important training technique which can help beginning counselors, regardless of theoretical orientation, bridge the gap between classroom learning and initial applied experiences. Within this framework, microcounseling should be viewed not as a training alternative but as a supplement to existing training programs.

Since the appearance of the introductory microcounseling article (Ivey *et al.*, 1968) there have been a number of significant studies which have expanded the number of skills that have been sufficiently identified to be discriminated, described, and modeled. Thus, not only does the microcounseling model add a new dimension to training but it has also served to stimulate attempts to identify actual counselor behaviors and to break what has previously been considered extremely complex behaviors into an increasing number of discrete, identifiable behaviors. A number of recent studies have suggested that microcounseling, in addition to being an effective training technique with beginning counselors and interviewers, may also be an effective therapy tool for helping clients acquire more effective interpersonal skills.

Chapter Three

ATTENDING BEHAVIOR: AN UNDERLYING CONSTRUCT OF MICROTRAINING

$\mathbf{M}$ ICROTRAINING PROCEDURES focus on specific skills and behaviors which can be defined, seen in operation, practiced, and
evaluated. Rather than confuse the interviewing trainee with an
overwhelming amount of data, the component-skills approach
breaks interviewing into workable and observable dimensions.

The basic question asked by the research team (Ivey,
Normington, Miller, Morrill, Haase, 1968) who first explored
this area was What are the specific component skills of counsel
ing? The search for skills to teach within the microcounseling
framework began in traditional interviewing, counseling, and
therapeutic texts. Many descriptions and theories were examined,
but none were sufficiently specific or behavioral to be taught as a
microtraining skill. The search next centered on direct observation of interviews, but these original efforts in observation proved
fruitless. It was easy to rate an interviewer as "good" or "bad"
but almost impossible to decide on what behaviors were indica-
tive of effective counselors.

The breakthrough which resulted in the concept of attending
behavior occurred with one of our secretaries, whom we shall
call Mary. Frustrated with our lack of success in identifying
skills of counseling, we decided to teach some interviewing skills
to our secretary who was unfamiliar with counseling procedures.
Mary was asked to talk with a volunteer client and attempt to
interview him; the session was to be videotaped. Mary began
with "What's your name? Where are you from? What year in
school are you?" The client responded pleasantly and positively,
but after he answered the third question, an awkward pause
occurred. Mary appeared tense and uncomfortable in her chair,

her eyes wandered about the room as she searched for something new to say. Shortly, she dredged up a new question and the interview proceded for a short time until another awkward break occurred. The interview continued in this stilted fashion for the remainder of the five-minute session. On only one occasion did Mary seem at ease; the client asked her a question and Mary momentarily forgot herself, relaxed and talked about herself. While this may be appropriate social behavior, it is generally not considered interviewing.*

Mary illustrated many of the behaviors of the beginning counselor. She focused on herself and her responsibility for conducting the interview to the extent that it was almost impossible for her to listen to the client. Awkward pauses, loss of eye contact, physical tension, and talking about oneself rather than listening have been noted as common characteristics of the beginning interviewer.

After the first five-minute session, Mary received impromptu microcounseling training. While no written manual describing what was to be called attending behavior was available, we talked with her about finding a more comfortable, relaxed position and maintaining eye contact with the client so that she could communicate attentiveness and interest. Mary was instructed not to add new topics, but simply to ask questions or make comments concerning something the client had already said. A videotape of experienced counselors was shown to Mary stressing these three concepts: (a) a relaxed, attentive posture, (b) eye contact, and (c) verbal following. Mary then viewed a videotape of the first session and analyzed her performance with the help of the supervisors. It might be observed that when we saw Mary failing to exhibit specific interviewing behaviors, it became possible to identify and teach them to her.

Following the training session, Mary returned to reinterview the same client. After a brief moment of artificiality, Mary began to respond in highly impactful ways. In fact, she looked like a highly skilled, experienced counselor. The change was not only

---

* However, later research and evaluation suggest that talking about oneself at appropriate times may be a most useful interviewing skill (Higgins, Ivey, and Uhlemann, 1970).

dramatic, but when we began to consider the twenty minutes of training it was almost shocking! We have had less change of behavior in some practicum students in an entire year. A pause occurred when the student had exhausted the last question, and Mary's lack of training in counseling skills again became apparent; however, after a short struggle, she asked a question regarding something that had been said earlier in the session, then relaxed, and the interview continued smoothly.

Interestingly, the behaviors learned in the interview generalized to other situations. The following Monday, Mary could not wait to tell us about attending to people over the weekend. She had developed a new behavioral repertoire which was reinforced by a new kind of excitement and involvement with other people.

ATTENTION AS POTENT REINFORCER

An important aspect of establishing a relationship with the client is being aware of, and responsive to, the communications of that individual and communicating this attentiveness. The communication of attentiveness is a potent reinforcer in counselor-client interaction and plays an important role in the establishment of a relationship. Skinner in *Science and Human Behavior* (1953, p. 78) has discussed the concepts of attention as follows:

> The attention of people is reinforcing because it is a necessary condition for other reinforcements for them. In general, only people who are attending to us reinforce our behavior. The attention of someone who is particularly likely to supply reinforcement—a parent, a teacher, or a loved one—is an especially good generalized reinforcer and sets up especially strong attention-getting behavior.

The research literature strongly supports the value of attention in promoting human behavior change. For example, Allen, Hart, Buell, Harris, and Wolf (1964) demonstrated that teacher attention was maintaining the peer isolation of a nursery school pupil. When the teachers switched their approach to giving the child attention when she was interacting with other children but not when she approached the teachers, her isolation behavior disappeared. Kennedy and Thompson (1967) used attention to modify the behavior of a hyperactive first-grade child. Whitley

and Sulzer (1970) used attention to help teachers reduce disruptive classroom behavior. Wahler (1969) has trained parents
in the use of differential attention to shape the behavior of
"oppositional children." Similar approaches in the use of attention with children have proven equally effective (Quay, Werry,
McQueen, and Sprague, 1966; Zimmerman and Zimmerman,
1962).

Evidence for the use of attention as a reinforcer of *verbal
behavior* was first provided by Greenspoon (1951) when he
successfully demonstrated that a subject's speech may be modified by minimal nonverbal and verbal cues. Extensive research
since that time has demonstrated a wide variety of methods
through which human behavior may be modified by verbal and
nonverbal attention patterns. Excellent reviews of the literature
in this field are provided by Bandura (1969), Phillips and Kanfer
(1969), and Ullmann and Krasner (1965).

Content analysis of interview typescripts reveals that counselors either directly or unconsciously selectively condition client
responses to suit the counselor's theoretical orientation (Bandura,
Lipher, and Miller, 1960; Murray, 1956; Rogers, 1960). Bandura
(1961, p. 154) has noted the following:

> . . . the results of these studies show that the therapist not only
> controls the patient by rewarding him with interest and approval
> when the patient behaves in a fashion the therapist desires but that
> he also controls through punishment in the form of mild disapproval
> and withdrawal of interest when the patient behaves in ways that
> are threatening to the therapist or run counter to his goals.

A BEHAVIORAL EXAMINATION OF ATTENTION

Despite the emphasis on attention as a generalized reinforcer,
relatively little thought has been given to the definition of the
behavioral components of attending. The three behaviors identified with Mary and subsequently studied by Ivey, Normington,
Miller, Morrill, and Haase (1968) are considered important by
others as well. The following discussion provides a framework
wherein the behavioral aspects of attention may be systematically
considered.

Pepyne and Zimmer (1969) have given special attention to

integrating *verbal conditioning and the counseling interview.* In their review, they conclude that counseling appears to be emerging as a process in which specific changes in a client's verbal behavior can be predicted as well as explained. Kennedy and Zimmer (1968) found that a paraphrase and a neutrally toned "mm-hmm" utterance were effective reinforcers with respect to self-reference statements; however, "mm-hmm" with an affirming head nod and "I see" were not. They also found that different counselors obtained significantly different results from comparable subjects. This work has been extended by Crowley (1970), Hackney (1969), and Pepyne (1968), who have further demonstrated specific aspects of the conditionability of response classes (topics) in the interview and emotionally laden and nonfeeling-tone statements.

Physical components of attending behavior also have a research background which justify their importance. *Nonverbal communication* patterns have recently shown themselves to be amenable to direct study (Duncan, 1969). Condon and Ogston (1966) have demonstrated that the physical movements of one member of a group or dyad affect others. Birdwhistell (1967) and Scheflen (1969) have demonstrated the possibility of systematizing body postures and shown the importance of nonverbal communication in interpersonal relationships.

A variety of studies have considered the importance of *eye contact* and visual interaction patterns. Exline has studied sex differences in eye-contact patterns (Exline, Gray, and Schuette, 1965; Exline and Winters, 1965) and has found that competitive and "Machiavellian" subjects tend to maintain eye contact longer under stressful conditions. Wardwell (1960) found that children tended to be very conscious of people looking at them, even though they might be involved in a task. In reviewing these and other studies, Duncan (1969, p. 131) notes the consistency in the research and concludes that, "This sort of consistency, if it continues to be encountered with subsequent studies, strongly suggests a high degree of regularity and organization. . . ."

Individuals give attention to one another by a variety of

means. While these can be divided into a variety of conceptual frameworks, the concepts of attending behavior (eye contact, physical attention, and verbal following behavior) appear to be central aspects by which people relate to, reinforce, and interact with one another. This brief summary of the research literature suggests the power of these means of interpersonal influence. Effectively combining the three dimensions into one larger construct would seem to provide an important vehicle for describing much of what happens between individuals in the interview, and in many of life's other interactions.

Attention is central to the interaction between interviewer and client. Unless the interviewer listens or attends to the client, little in the way of understanding will occur. Too many beginning counselors and interviewers fail to listen to their clients.

Attending behavior coupled with microtraining techniques offers a new approach to many problems. Attending can be taught as technique, but unlike pure technique ("say the client's name at least three times") attending implies real interaction. In order to engage in the skill of attending to client comments, the person must listen to content. To follow communication of feeling by appropriate changes in voice timbre and quality and by appropriate statements, one must attend to the feeling that is being communicated. The person who is incongruent or attending to himself rather than the client will be unable to listen. Once it is initiated, attending seems self-reinforcing and many even provide an approach that can be used regardless of the theoretical framework or applied work situation of the trainee.

Some may question the possible artificiality of attending behavior or other skills suggested in this book. They validly object to seeing life as a series of exercises in which the individual constantly dredges into a "handbag of skills" so he can adapt to each life situation. Our experience has been that individuals may sometimes begin attending in an artificial, deliberate manner. However, once attending has been initiated, the person to whom one is listening tends to become more animated, and this in turn reinforces the attender who very quickly forgets about attending deliberately and soon attends naturally. A variety of our clients and trainees have engaged in conscious attending behavior only to find themselves so interested in the person with whom they are talking that they lose themselves in the other.

Polanyi's (1966) concept of tacit knowing discussed in Chapter One provides a useful explanation of this phenomenon. As in the golf swing of the talented professional, the specific behaviors of attention have been integrated (unconsciously if you will) into a larger, perhaps more meaningful gestalt. Sparking deliberate and distinct behavioral acts into a new whole is the relationship (or mutual reinforcement pattern) between the individual who first started attending and the person to whom he attended. Koestler (1964) describes similar phenomena under the concept of the habit hierarchy and points out that the bringing together of formerly distinct behaviors into a new whole frees the individual for creative exploration of larger and more complex issues.

In summary, attending behavior could be defined as simple listening. However, the three central aspects of attending behavior provide a specific set of behaviors through which listening may be taught. Too often interviewer trainers have said "listen," without defining what the act of listening is. The counselor should look at his client to note postural movements, gestures, and facial expressions which give important indications concerning the client. Eye contact need not be constant, nor should it be fixed staring; it should be natural looking at the client. Secondly, postural position and relaxation are important. Unless the interviewer is relaxed, he will find it difficult to focus on the client. When a person is tense in an interviewing session, his attention may be focused on himself rather than his client.

Finally, verbal following behavior demands that the counselor respond to the last comment or some preceding comment of the client without introducing new data. Topic jumping or asking questions in a random pattern is a common occurrence among beginning interviewers. If the interviewer attends to the client's comments and does not add new information, it is surprising how well he gets to know his client. In our society, few people really listen to one another; when someone attends to us, it is a powerful reinforcer to keep talking.

ATTENDING, ISLAND, AND HIATUS BEHAVIOR*

Audiotapes of counseling sessions have tended to give the impression that the counseling interview is a continuous process. With video-recording, the counseling session is not seen as a continuous unit but as a series of island and hiatuses.

The island consists of a topic (response class) or a series of very closely related topics, sometimes small, sometimes broad in nature. The island is clearly a unit, and there is almost complete agreement among observers of a tape of the point where the counselor and client reach the end of an island. At this point, a hiatus occurs, a pause or respite. The hiatus may be very short or it may be extended; it may be represented by the uncomfortable period where the novice therapist desperately searches for something to say while his client anxiously awaits another go-ahead signal or it may be a comfortable period of reflection between an experienced therapist and his patient in the midst of profitable long-term therapy.

The hiatus appears to be a period of negotiation between the counselor and client, a negotiation in which new response classes or topics are sought. Both counselor and client become acutely aware of both verbal and nonverbal cues during this negotiation. The client in search of a new topic may present possible alternatives to which the therapist has the choice of attending or ignoring (reinforcing or extinguishing). A typescript of this type of interaction might read as follows:

Client: Well, I can't think of anything else to say.
Interviewer: (Silence.)
Client: I think I'll go shopping this afternoon.
Interviewer: (Silence.)
Client: Except I don't like to go shopping alone and all my friends have classes this afternoon.
Interviewer: It's not fun to do things alone.

In this example, possible topics (shopping, class schedule, friends, and being alone) are treated differently by the counselor.

------

* This section is rewritten from a paper "Attending, Island, and Hiatus Behavior" in the *Journal of Counseling Psychology* (Hackney, Ivey, and Oetting, 1970).

By his silence, he extinguished certain topics. When he does reinforce the client's last comment by attending, he selects the potentially loaded topic of lack of companionship. If the client responds to the counselor's statement, the negotiation, and thus the hiatus, is concluded, and a new island emerges.

The island, of course, represents a series of interviewer-client utterances on a similar topic. It appears to flow smoothly until that topic is exhausted and a new hiatus or negotiation takes place.

It is now possible to return to Mary, our secretarial interviewer-in-training. When a topic was launched and Mary was attending, she appeared almost as a professional counselor. However, when a hiatus was reached, her lack of training in counseling skills became apparent. The hiatus called for initiation of new areas, and Mary did not follow one of the counseling or interviewing traditions. If she had, she would have waited for the client to respond (nondirective), initiated an expression of her own feeling state (recent client-centered), directed attention to an early experience (analytic), presented a discriminative stimulus to elicit verbal responses which could be reinforced (learning theory), brought out a Strong Vocational Interest Blank (vocational counseling), or asked a question about previous job history (employment interviewing for job placement).

Mary actually began to talk about an interesting experience in her own immediate past (standard social behavior). However, since she was still attempting to engage in attending behavior, when the interviewee responded to her, she listened to him, reinforced his comment, and once again *looked like* the highly skilled interviewer.

The concepts of island and hiatus in interviewing provide useful speculations for research in counseling and therapy. Some of the contradictory research findings in content analysis of counseling may be explained with these terms. It is possible that those studies showing highly consistent counselor behaviors between theoretical disciplines have focused on behaviors characteristic of islands, and those studies showing differential behavior for counselors of differing persuasions have focused upon behaviors characteristic of the hiatus.

All successful interviewers, counselors, and therapists have basic attending skills. They are good listeners, are relaxed and natural in the interviewing session, maintain some type of consistent eye contact (in some cases, it is recognized that therapists avoid eye contact but still maintain attention), and verbally attend or follow through with clients.

However, it is equally clear that interviewers, counselors, and therapists of differing persuasions and differing skills do indeed differ. It is likely that they differ in what they attend to or reinforce in the client's behavior. An employment interviewer may notice the nonverbal cues of his interviewee but ignore them if they are not job-relevant, whereas an existential therapist may pay considerable attention to these same cues. An analyst may attend to statements about a person's work primarily in terms of analytic significance. The hiatus or negotiation period provides the clearest opportunity for observation and study of differential reinforcing or attending patterns of interviewers.

Attention might provide an explanation for the success of the many varieties of counseling and interviewing approaches. For example, it has been pointed out that an analytic client dreams in Freudian symbols, a Jungian client in mythological symbolism, and Gestalt client in parts and whole. It seems possible that the therapist at key hiatus points has simply selectively attended or reinforced the client's verbalizations which support his theoretical framework. A Freudian client may have a mythological symbol in his dream, but if his mention of the symbol is met by silence on the part of the therapist it is not likely to figure prominently in the session.

Similarly, vocational counselors demonstrate differential attending or reinforcement patterns. One counselor may attend primarily to past work history and factual information about job progression, noting and reinforcing client comments about skills and competencies developed. Another counselor may attend to client comments related to attitudes and emotions toward the supervisor. Thus, typescripts of vocational interviews conducted from different attentional frames would reveal marked differences in content, although both counselors might be very effective in attending behavior.

ATTENDING BEHAVIOR AND INTENTIONALITY

Ivey (1970) and Ivey and Rollin (in press) have discussed the *intentional individual,* the fully functioning person, in the following way:

> The person who acts with intentionality has a sense of capability. He is one who can generate alternative behaviors in a given situation and "come at" a problem from different vantage points. The intentional individual is not bound to one course of action but can respond in the moment to changing life situations as he looks forward to longer-term goals.

Microteaching in interviewing techniques draws on a similar concept. The beginning counselor often cannot act with intentionality; he does not have a sufficiently varied behavioral repertoire and so may tend to act in a stereotyped fashion, using one or two types of interview leads. Training in the specific skills of microcounseling gives the beginning counselor a series of specific behaviors which may be drawn on to facilitate interviewer-client interaction.

The model of the intentional interviewer supplies a general frame of reference for the objectives of an interviewing or counseling training program. Most interviewer trainers wish to help their trainees develop a unique approach to interviewing. While the supervisor may occasionally serve as a beginning model for the novice therapist, he is most effective when the trainee develops his own behavioral repertoire or interviewing style. The fully professional counselor is his own person. While he understands and appreciates the skills of others, he is capable of making his own unique synthesis in the actual interview.

The specific objective of microtraining is to supply the beginning counseling or interviewing trainee with an acquaintance of and experience in a variety of interviewing skills. It is anticipated that no one student needs, nor will be interested in, all the skills which could be taught. *Microcounseling, then, is concerned with introducing trainees to a variety of skills in expectation that each individual will eventually develop his own behavioral repertoire.*

Mary's behavior could also be viewed from the framework of intentionality. When the hiatus was reached during the first session, her behavioral repertoire as an interviewer was limited, perhaps nonexistent, and she had no readily available response. Hence the awkward pauses, talking about herself, and topic jumping. When Mary was given the one additional skill of attending behavior, response possibilities were greatly increased, the conversational islands lengthened, she talked less, and the individual with whom she was talking enjoyed the session more.

As one swallow does not make a summer, neither does attending behavior make an interviewer. Additional skills, practice, and experience would be necessary before Mary could demonstrate fully effective interviewing techniques. Mary's intentionality as an interviewer was increased by adding attending behavior to her repertoire, but it would require more skills to give her more choices if she were to become fully intentional. One cannot be free or make choices unless one has alternatives available.

Then what is the relationship between attending behavior and intentionality? The interviewer's use of attending behavior in the interview determines the direction and content of the session. Zimmer and his students (Crowley, 1970; Hackney, 1969; Pepyne, 1968) and Miller, *et al.* (1969) demonstrated that selective attention or reinforcement profoundly influence what happens in the interview. Through his use of attention and the constructs of attending behavior, the intentional counselor can lead the interview in many directions. Through use of selective attention and a variety of behavioral skills, the counselor may be of maximal benefit to a maximum number and types of clients. The one-tool counselor who may lack intentionality, the ability to direct his attention, and accompanying behavioral skills is less flexible and less able to deal with new and unusual occurrences during interviews. Further, the range of clients to whom he may be of benefit is reduced. He is unable to attend to the variety of responses and behaviors the client emits. As such, he is unable to respond to all dimensions of the individual's experience.

ATTENDING BEHAVIOR, ATTENTION, AND OTHER FRAMES OF REFERENCE

Attending behavior is considered here primarily from a behavioral frame of reference. The related construct of attention has been an issue in psychology for a considerable period of time. There are important distinctions between attending behavior and attention as the following definition by William James (1890, pp. 403-404) illustrates:

> Everyone knows what attention is. It is the taking possession by the mind, in clear and vivid form, of one out of what seems several possible objects or trains of thought. Focalization, concentration, of consciousness are of its essence. It implies withdrawal from some things in order to deal effectively with others, and it is a condition which has a real opposite in the confused, dazed, scatterbrained state which in French is called *distraction* . . .

Attention appears to describe the functional significance of attending behavior in that it is a way in which the conscious organization of experience may be described. Much of Luria's (1969) work describing the development of cerebral organization in children could be viewed from a similar frame of reference, although he does not emphasize the term "attention."

Attending behavior is directly observable and measurable, while attention remains a more subtle area of study. It is possible, for example, for an interviewer to be engaging in attending behavior in terms of all physical and verbal manifestations while his primary attention is directed elsewhere. The Skinnerian view of attention is one which is best observed in the behavioral relationship of one individual to another. The focus of attention as described by William James, however, remains a more intuitive, inner-directed matter, less subject to direct observation.

The literature on attention has been diverse and has demonstrated a lack of synthesis over the years. Woodworth and Schlosberg (1954, pp. 72-73) made the following comment:

> In spite of the practical reality of attending, the status of attention in systematic psychology has been uncertain and dubious for a long time. Early psychologists thought of it as a faculty or power, akin to the Will. . . . Any such view was strongly opposed by the associationists who wished to recognize as forces only sensory stimulations and association. The Gestalt psychologists have regarded any force of attention as extraneous to the field forces which in their view are the dynamic factors in human activity. The behaviorists have rejected attention as a mere traditional mentalistic concept.

Recently, however, attention has been examined in more depth. Norman (1969) has developed a comprehensive model for attentional processes and presents valuable data on selective attention, the acquisition and processing of information, and memory. Trabasso and Bower (1968) have studied the relationship of attention to learning. Both works summarize much of the literature on attention. A major symposium on attention was held at the 1969 International Congress of Psychology in London. The recent review by Swets and Kristofferson (1970) should also be cited. It appears that attention as a construct is gaining increasing popularity.

Attention is also an important construct in more esoteric areas of psychology. Maupin (1965), for example, examined the concept of attention in relationship to Zen meditation exercise. Kasamatsu and Hirai (1966) found that the focused attention of Zen exercises resulted in predictable patterns of brain-wave alpha rhythm. Shor (1962) relates hypnosis to concepts of attention. Diekman (1963) discusses mystical phenomena as being founded initially on focused attention and cites hypnotic concepts of automatization similar to the integrative constructs of Polanyi (1966) and Koestler (1964) mentioned earlier. Discussing autogenic training, Luthe (1963) describes many studies in which passive concentration, special types of attention, and related methods have resulted in drops in blood sugar, decreases in muscle potential, changes in peripheral circulation, rise in skin temperature, respiratory changes, and other physical phenomena. Instruction in such inner attentional processes may someday become part of every person's experience.

Attention and existentialism also deserve consideration. The French *distraction* described by William James as a confused, disordered state is closely akin to Roquentin's experience of decomposition in the following passage from Sartre's *Nausea* (1964, p. 128):

> Existence is a deflection. Trees, night-blue pillars, the happy bubbling of a fountain, vital smells, little heat mists floating in the cold air, a red-haired man digesting on a bench . . . In vain I tried to *count* the chestnut trees, to *locate* them by their relationship to the Velleda, to compare their height with the height of the plane

trees: each of them escaped the relationship in which I tried to enclose it, isolated itself, and overflowed.

It may be observed that the inability of Roquentin to focus on or attend to his surroundings has been important in his inability to organize his world. Similarly, the inability of the three principals to commit themselves to action in *No Exit* (Sartre, 1946) is another powerful description of the inability of man to maintain attention or commitment to his environment in a focal manner. It is interesting to observe that participants in sensory-restriction experiments tend to experience problems of attention not unlike those described above (Zubec, 1964a, 1964b, 1964c). Understimulation appears to produce a similar problem in developing consistent attentional processes.

The French existentialists suggest that the way out of man's dilemma is action in an absurd world despite possible awareness that the action itself may be absurd. The route to action is existential commitment—or alternatively defined, the focalization of one's attentional processes to one dimension of the multitude of possibilities which exist in one's environment. The analogy between the existential paradox "to live is to die" and the need for withdrawal from other stimuli if one is to concentrate on one stimulus in James' definition should be apparent.

Intentionality is, of course, a concept prominent in the writing of some existentialists (May, 1969). The more behavioral definition of intentionality presented here may not be much different from that of the self-actualized individual. The truly effective or actualized interviewer will have many alternative behaviors open to him and the capability to engage in these behaviors with satisfaction to himself and others. The concepts of intentionality, attending behavior, and attention suggest some areas of agreement, or at least discussion, between differing views of man.

Conscious, deliberate attending behavior may be viewed as one route out of the existential dilemma. Consider the beginning interviewer beleaguered by a multitude of stimuli from his talkative client. He may be unable to organize or synthesize any meaning from his client's comments. Clearly the client is in control of such a session (even though he may be seeking help from the counselor). The counselor who supplies a variety of leads and responses to the client without any effort at organization may confuse himself and the client. By deliberate focusing on one dimension of the client's experience, the counselor can help bring the interview under control; and once the interview has been focused, it is possible to build gradually to the most important and relevant dimensions and to help the client grow.

SUMMARY

Attention and the accompanying constructs of attending behavior provide a comprehensive framework for the intentional interviewer. Counselors of varying orientations and areas of expertise may be distinguished by the issues of content and feeling to which they attend and thus reinforce. As such, attending behavior does not explain varying counseling theories nor does it suggest that one type of interviewing is more effective than another. Attending behavior simply illustrates an important common denominator in a variety of counseling and interviewing approaches. It also provides a systematic way to test the validity of alternative approaches.

More than one approach to human behavior change is effective. At a minimum, there is clinical evidence indicating that approaches as varying as psychoanalysis, trait-factor vocational counseling, and behavior therapy do assist individuals. The important question may be which therapist, with what treatment is most appropriate, at what time, with what important situational variables, and with what client? If this highly individualistic approach to interviewing and behavior change is accepted, the intentional counselor, who is able to direct his response in a variety of directions, may well be the most successful individual.

Chapter Four

THE COMPONENT SKILLS OF
MICROCOUNSELING

M ICROTRAINING TECHNIQUES are based on a component-skills approach. Allen and Ryan (1969) point out that identifying and teaching single skills enables the learner to understand, practice, and develop proficiency in many areas before he moves into the more complex world of actual practice. The individual who has developed a repertoire of interviewing skills and knows what effects these skills have on others is equipped for his first counseling sessions. Further, he has a method through which he can grow further.

While a number of interviewing skills are outlined in this chapter, they should be seen as only one view of the organization and the nature of skills involved in the processes of counseling, interviewing, and therapy. Those with a behavioral orientation may find attending behavior and its many possible variations most valid; reflection of feeling and summarization skills may prove most related to nondirective and client-centered orientations, and adaptions of interpretation skills may be most relevant to dynamically oriented individuals. Further, the skills suggested here may be reconceptualized or rejected by some readers, especially those who might disagree with the emphasis throughout on attending behavior and attentional processes.

Microcounseling is an open system; the skills presented here are only an indication of the possible uses for the microtraining paradigm. Those who test the microcounseling framework can adapt and modify existing skills and add new concepts of their own. We have found that microcounseling is most meaningful and effective when the individual uses it in his own manner.

This chapter describes twelve skills of interviewing which

51

have thus far been identified and experimentally and clinically tested. The skills are organized into the following related groups: skills useful in beginning interviews, listening skills, interpretation, and skills of self-expression; a final section explores means to integrate skills into broader problems and issues in the interview.

BEGINNING SKILLS OF INTERVIEWING

Studies of novice interviewer behavior by Matarazzo, Phillips, Wiens, and Saslow (1965); Matarazzo, Wiens, and Saslow (1966); and Phillips and Matarazzo (1962) have revealed that novice interviewers tend to make many communication errors. Most notably, beginners frequently cut off interaction with their clients by asking closed-ended questions or by making long, awkward speeches. When one speaks with novices after these sessions, they often report that they were most uncomfortable and could not get the client to talk. Stories of errors made by beginning interviewers and novice therapists are legion. Most of these problems can be traced to the fact that the beginner simply did not know what to do and did not have a beginning behavioral repertoire to rely on when awkward moments or hiatuses appeared.

It seems necessary and helpful to equip the neophyte counselor or interviewer with some survival skills so that his first sessions are not disastrous to him or his client. Patterson (1968) explores this issue in detail. He cites evidence indicating that counseling or psychotherapy can lead to client damage even when practiced by experienced counselors or therapists. Thus, the importance of providing new interviewers with interviewing skills cannot be denied. Three beginning skills are suggested here. These are attending behavior, open invitation to talk, and minimal encourages.

Attending Behavior

Attending behavior is a basic skill underlying many dimensions of counseling. It has been taught to a wide variety of individuals, including advanced clinical psychology graduate students, paraprofessionals and fourth graders, with success. It is an especially clear skill, can be taught to individuals or small groups, and is easily learned in a one-hour period.

Attending behavior serves many functions for the beginning interviewer. The experience of success and seeing oneself improve rapidly is highly reinforcing. For more sophisticated trainees, attending behavior can be presented as an introductory skill, one which will enable them to become acquainted with the microtraining format and see themselves on television for the first time.

Most important, attending behavior gives a trainee something to do when he simply does not know what to do in the session. In such awkward moments, the interviewer can simply maintain eye contact, retain a relaxed, easy body posture, think back to something that interested him in the client's earlier discussion, make a comment about it, and the interview then can proceed. One of the most important skills that the advanced therapist or personnel interviewer has when he feels pressed in the interview is the ability to relax, reflect on the session, and then respond to the client in some appropriate fashion. One cannot help but think of the many interviewers who have used their pipes as a method to put themselves together before responding to the client.

For those who are oriented to behavioral approaches in the interview, a wide variety of adaptations and extensions of the use of attending behavior as a reinforcer are feasible. Following a model suggested by the studies of Crowley (1970), Hackney (1969), and Pepyne (1968), it would be possible to develop microcounseling skills in which trainees would demonstrate their ability to alternately reinforce various types of affective and cognitive content. For example, trainees could demonstrate their ability to reinforce emotional comments about parents. This then could be extinguished through lack of attention, and then again reinforced. The beginning or experienced counselor who demonstrates this type of control in the session might be expected to gain considerable confidence in his ability to handle difficult situations. A variety of skills using attention as a reinforcer can be developed to allow trainees to sharpen their ability to shape client behavior in a multitude of directions.

At another level, attending behavior can be viewed more simply as listening thoughtfully to another person. An emphasis on being with the client, hearing him thoroughly, and noting his experience, when coupled with attending behavior training in microcounseling, can lead to a phenomenological or existential orientation. In dynamic orientations, attending behavior could best be considered a general listening skill, primarily used by the therapist to gain information.

Attending behavior's main components of eye contact, physical posture, and verbal following behavior can be taught separately if a trainee is functioning at a low level. In teaching some mental patients the concepts of attending behavior, we have found that teaching three concepts simultaneously may be too demanding. Similarly, some interviewing trainees may need special advice and assistance in developing appropriate eye contact patterns or physical attending behaviors, especially if they demonstrate unusual patterns in their interviews.

Open Invitation to Talk

This skill, which was developed by Phillips, Lockhart, and Moreland (1969b), is specifically concerned with teaching the beginning interviewer to ask open-ended questions and encourage the client to talk and explore his thoughts and feelings. An open invitation is best understood when compared with a closed approach to interviewing:

> *Open*: Could you tell me a little bit about your last job?
> How did you feel about your wife's ignoring you?
> *Closed*: Did you like your last job?
> Do you get angry with your wife's ignoring you?

Phillips, Lockhart, and Moreland observe that open comments provide *room* for client exploration without categories being imposed by the interviewer. An open invitation to talk allows the client many alternatives for self-expression. The closed question, on the other hand, tends to be factual and can often be answered with a yes or no. Interviews focusing on closed questions often give the client a feeling of interrogation. Employment interviews which stress past job history, educational background, and related factual information represent a prime example of closed communication. In such sessions, the interviewer fails to obtain a real understanding of important attitudes, feelings, and experiences of the applicant or employee which might be vital to eventual placement.

In summarizing open invitation to talk, Phillips, Lockhart, and Moreland (1969b, p. 1) conclude the following:

> Crucial to the giving of open-ended questions is the concept of who is to lead the interview. While the interviewer does ask questions while using this skill, his questions are centered around concerns of the client rather than around concerns of the interviewer for the client. Questions should be designed to help the client clarify his own problems, rather than provide information for the interviewer. . . . If the interviewer relies on closed questions to structure his interview, he usually is forced to concentrate so hard on thinking up the next question that he fails to listen to and attend to the client.

Open invitation to talk may be viewed as an extension of attending behavior in that it directs attention to the client's needs and wishes rather than to those of the interviewer. By focusing attention on the client's communication, it becomes possible to understand him and his ideas more fully.

Phillips, Lockhart, and Moreland point out additional values of open invitation to be considered. They assist the beginning counselor start an interview ("How have things been on the job these past few days?" as opposed to, "Is your job going well?"). They may be used to help the client give specific examples of behavior so that the interviewer is better able to understand what is being described ("Could you give me an example of what you mean when you say you don't get along with your roommate?"). Finally, open invitations can be especially useful in helping the client focus his attention on emotions ("What are you feeling as we talk about this?" as compared to, "Do you feel anxious now?").

However, closed questions are also appropriate at times. Closed questions used appropriately, following an extended rambling discourse, can help the client focus his attention on central issues. Then, when the client has a "fix" or focus around which he can think, open invitation to talk may again be utilized. The skilled interviewer uses a balance between open and closed questions to facilitate the growth of his client; varying types of interviews will obviously require differing proportions of open versus closed interview leads.

Minimal Encourages to Talk

This skill is concerned with helping the client to keep talking once he has started to talk. Some beginning counselors are effective at using attending behavior and open invitations to get clients talking but then lapse into nonparticipation, failing to encourage the client to keep going. Minimal encourages to talk, also developed by Phillips, Lockhart, and Moreland (1969a), focus on helping the trainee become more active and involved in the session while remaining centered on the client's needs and wishes.

Examples of minimal encourages include simply an "um-hmm," repetitions of one or two words from what the client has just said, one word questions, head nods, and a variety of body postures and gestures. By using such minimal encourages, the interviewer is showing interest and involvement, but is allowing the client to determine the primary direction of the interview. More advanced trainees may wish to study the use of minimal encourages in detail.

Minimal encourages also serve as important reinforcers for client behavior. The integration of minimal encourages with reinforcement concepts helps the behavioral counselor direct the interview more effectively. Those of a phenomenological bent often use minimal encourages as a manifestation of their involvement, interest, and caring for the client.

Phillips, Lockhart, and Moreland stress that "the successful usage of this technique presupposes that the interviewer has tuned into what the client is discussing." Randomly encouraging the client to talk will not facilitate either the growth of the client or the direction of the interview. Minimal encourages should follow directly from what the client has said. In this way, they can help the client express himself more clearly and provide an avenue whereby the counselor or interviewer can express his interest in the client and assist him in continued self-exploration.

LISTENING SKILLS: SELECTIVE ATTENTION

Once the beginning counselor can attend, can open the client to talk and encourage him to continue, the question of direction or focus for the interview then becomes paramount. To what should the interviewer attend? What should he encourage the client to talk about? How can he help the client explore himself in more depth?

Skinner (1953) suggests that attention in itself is not a sufficient reinforcer for human beings. He indicates that approval is another generalized reinforcer which may be used to shape the behavior of others. "Another person is likely to reinforce only that part of one's behavior of which he approves, and any sign of his approval becomes reinforcing in its own right" (p. 78). The literature on verbal conditioning suggests that individuals in interviewing sessions will respond and talk about areas in which the counselor responds to and reinforces.

This section discusses two central aspects of focused listening. These are reflections or responding to feeling and the paraphrase, which focuses on cognitive content of the session. These concepts are discussed as microtraining skills and a presentation is made of two additional broader interviewing skills—summarization of feeling and the summative paraphrase.

Reflection and Summarization of Feeling

Attending behavior could be described as being with the client physically and verbally. The construct of reflection of feeling (Rogers, 1961) is often viewed as related to empathy or being with the client. It could be also described as *selective attention to the feeling* or emotional aspects of the client's expressions. By selectively attending and reflecting observed feeling states to the client, the interviewer is consciously reinforcing emotional states while simultaneously extinguishing more cognitive aspects by ignoring them.

Accurate reflection of feeling was the second skill focused on by microcounseling research. Originally developed by Normington (Ivey *et al.*, 1968), this skill was chosen because of the important part it can play, in Rogerian terminology, in communicating to the client that "I am with you . . . I can accurately sense the world as you are feeling and perceiving it." Such communication is considered important in the development of empathic understanding, a key aspect of an effective interpersonal relationship.

The following client statement and examples of possible interviewer responses illustrates how selective attention may explain and help make operational the sometimes mystical concept of reflection of feelings.

> *Client*: So I'm wondering if you can help me find a new major.
> *Counselor*: (Silence.)
> *Client*: I suppose if I did find one, I'd just bungle things again.
> *Counselor*: You feel discouraged;
>   *or*
> You feel that it's pretty futile to try again.

Both of the suggested alternatives focus on feeling and emotional states and tend to ignore cognitive aspects of the client's communication. If followed by further emotional reflection, the client may move to depth exploration of his feelings of inadequacy. The statements above may vary in quality, but both selectively attend to emotional aspects of the client's comment.

Alternatively, selective attention to cognitive content (paraphrasing) could help change the direction of the same session. Counselor comments selectively attending to other aspects of client communication would lead in other directions. Examples of this might include "You'd like me to help you" (leading to discussions of possible dependency and the counselor-client relationship). The open invitation to talk, "What majors have you considered?" is another alternative which opens the individual to a different type of exploration (redirects attention to the issue of future directions and may lead to discussion of future alternatives).

In this comparison, reflection of feeling becomes clearer.

The task of the interviewer is to note emotional aspects of the client's comments and summarize them in clear form so that the client himself may better understand them. In this view, the value of the Rogerian mirror becomes more clear. The most skillful reflection of feeling is the one which is attuned to the client's present emotions. This is easily distinguished from cognitive content or substantive questions raised in other portions of the same interview.

The third microcounseling study designed by Normington and Miller (Ivey, *et al.*, 1968) focused on summarization of feeling. Summarization involves attending to the client, accurately sensing the feelings which are being expressed, and meaningfully integrating the various responses of the client. Summarization of feeling is seen as an extension of attending behavior and reflection of feeling. However, in this case, the counselor is attending to a broader class of client response and must have the skill to bring together seemingly diverse elements into a meaningful gestalt.

Summarization of feeling could be described by possible counselor responses in an interview in which a client expresses many different feelings and attitudes toward his employer. Attention to feelings will help this client express himself freely and more fully. However, after a period of time, many diverse positive and negative elements of emotion will have been expressed. In addition, the interviewer may have observed nonverbal communications of the client which strengthen his understanding of the client's overall emotional state regarding the supervisor. A summarization-of-feeling response is exemplified by summarizing and pointing out the diverse and complex feelings of the client in such a way that the client may say, "That's *right*, I never looked at it that way before," and continues on with his discussion of the issue.

In the example cited above, the interviewer seeks to attend and selectively reinforce client comments and behavior in such a fashion that an overall picture of the client's various feelings is obtained. The counselor then integrates these specific behavioral observations into a gestalt or total picture which can be summarized for the client. A summarization of feeling is judged effective only in relationship to the client's reception and use of that same summarization. If the client is overwhelmed by too much data or the summarization is too simple and obvious, it will not facilitate further client exploration.

Virtually all interviewers, counselors, and therapists reflect or summarize their client's feelings from time to time. The personnel interviewer, perhaps interested in a job applicant's attitudes toward a stressful executive post, finds it helpful to reflect feeling states for better understanding of the applicant. In turn, he may use this same information to help the applicant understand himself more fully. Most counselors and therapists use reflection-of-feeling statements from time to time, although the emphasis and number of statements of this type vary with theoretical persuasion.

Much of interviewing is centered on feelings and emotions. Selective attention to emotions as taught through the microcounseling framework provides a useful conceptual tool to help the beginning interviewer develop the skills of reflection and summarization of feelings.

Occasionally, reflection of feeling proves too complex a skill for a beginning trainee to learn readily. Haase, Forsyth, Julius, and Lee (1969) have developed and tested the microtraining skill of "expression of feeling." In their model, beginning counselors first learn how to recognize and express their own emotions before they practice reflection of feeling. Working with subprofessional counselors, Haase and DiMattia (1970) found that training in expression of feeling facilitated later growth in reflection-of-feeling skills.

Paraphrasing and the Summative Paraphrase

Paraphrasing, a technique used by all interviewers, could be considered an attempt to feed back to the client the content of what he has just said, but in a restated form. Used in this manner, this skill, developed by Ivey, Moreland, Phillips, and Lockhart (1969), is functional in clarifying confusing verbal content, tying a number of recent comments together, and highlighting issues by stating them more concisely.

Paraphrasing is a variation of selective attention. Paraphrasing is a skill designed to help the counselor and client clarify what is said through selective attention to objective verbal content. Paraphrasing centers more on cognitive than affective components. Just as reflection of feeling entails some reiteration of content, so paraphrasing entails some recognition of the client's feeling. The primary distinction is emphasis.

Paraphrasing could also be termed "restatement of content" and is the interviewer lead most often associated with the jokes sometimes made about nondirective counselors. Typescripts containing many paraphrases have sometimes been criticized as simple repetition of what the client has just said. Paraphrases at their worst do indeed represent mere repetition.

Good paraphrases, however, require the interviewer to reflect to the client the essence of his last comment or last few comments. If the paraphrase helps the client move further and talk more deeply about the subject at hand, it may be considered a successful lead. Whereas reflection and summarization of feeling can serve as a sufficient method for some counselors and therapists, skillful paraphrasing may serve as an adequate interview method for the job counselor, personnel director, or guidance counselor seeking a more complete understanding of a situation.

The distinction between paraphrasing and reflection of feeling is illustrated in the following examples:

Client: I don't know about him. One moment, he's nice as can be, and the next he treats me terribly.

Interviewer: He's pretty inconsistent, you don't know what to do. (Paraphrase.) You feel confused. (Reflection of feeling.)

Client: I'm afraid I will flunk my geometry course.

Interviewer: The geometry course is pretty rough. (Paraphrase.) You're worried. (Reflection of feeling.)

Both examples above provide the individuals with opportunities to keep exploring their problems. Reflection of feeling stresses emotional aspects of the client's communication, whereas paraphrasing stresses more objective content and the immediate problem to be faced, although allowing the individual to replace them with emotion if he wishes.

Parallel to summarization of feeling is the *summative para-phrase* in which the interviewer attends to and reflects back to the client the essence of a larger section of the interview. A summative paraphrase reviews the essential content of the session and may be particularly helpful to the client about to make a decision concerning action in vocational or personal areas. It also provides an opportunity to clarify confusing content, tie a number of comments together, highlight issues by stating them concisely, or check the interviewer's perception.

SKILLS OF SELF-EXPRESSION

The interviewing skills which have been presented thus far depend primarily on the ability of the counselor to listen and attend to the client. While these skills demand clinical judgment, the central focus is on determining what the client is really saying and helping him express himself more clearly. While attending skills are important, the beginning counselor must do more than listen and communicate that he is listening.

The interviewer must also learn to express himself and his ideas clearly and relevantly. The nondirective movement in counseling has fallen into disrepute in some quarters due to some of its adherents simply sitting back and never involving themselves with their clients. Rogers has recognized the importance of interviewers expressing themselves, and his emphasis on participation with others on a more open, honest basis is still increasing (e.g. Rogers, 1969).

This section considers an area of microtraining still in its conceptual beginnings. While four studies have been compiled using a variety of self-expression skills, it is believed that the potential of this area for growth and study may exceed that of attending skills. Skills of expression of feeling, exposition of content, and direct, mutual communication are explored.

Expression of Feeling

First used successfully by Haase, Forsyth, Julius and Lee (1969) to teach clients how to express their own feelings in a counseling interview more easily and directly, this skill has increasingly shown promise and importance as part of counselor training. In client-centered and existential-phenomenological psychology, the expression of counselor emotions is sometimes used as a facilitating dimension of the interview. For beginning counselors who have difficulty reflecting a client's feeling, direct training in expression of feeling may serve as valuable pretraining.

This skill is an analogue of reflection of feeling with the exception that the trainee places emphasis on his own feeling states and attitudes. Training in expression of feeling encourages the expression of emotions as opposed to cognitive content. A topic is selected and stress is placed on distinguishing feeling from emotion. The following is a typical example in which the trainee is attempting to discuss his feelings toward his high school teachers.

> *Expression of feeling*: I really liked Mr. Brown and Mr. Smith. They understood me. It made me feel good to walk into their classes. I really wanted to try hard for them.
>
> *Expression of content*: I had two good teachers in high school, Mr. Brown and Mr. Smith. I took physics and chemistry from them.

Many individuals when attempting to discuss their emotions will almost immediately revert to a discussion of objective content. Training in expression of feeling appears to facilitate self-expression.

Haase and DiMattia (1970) trained paraprofessionals in expression of feeling and found that it facilitated their learning reflection of feeling. They noted this skill helped trainees to "discriminate between content and affect, and to be able to accurately sense, identify and verbalize the affective component of a verbal message."

At more sophisticated levels, adaptions of the expression-of-feeling conceptions may prove useful in aiding client-centered or existential-phenomenological therapists express their own feeling states more relevantly in the interview. Not too long ago, expression of counselor attitudes was prohibited by much of counseling theory. With the change in emphasis, methods and training materials which stress counselor reactions in interviewing leads are needed.

Expression of Content

The clear expressions of findings and results are important in vocational-educational, personnel interviews, and presentations of diagnostic reports so that others can understand them. Miller, Morrill, and Uhlemann (1970), for example, have developed a general training program in test interpretation in which beginning counselors are taught several skills of communicating test results to clients. In their program, they used half-hour micro-training practice sessions in the belief that more complex skills require longer periods of time.

In a refinement of the above study, Miller, Morrill, Ivey, Normington, and Uhlemann (1969) taught beginning counselors the relatively specific skill of reinforcing clients' emotional attitudes toward psychological tests. One of the important skills of test interpretation is recognizing client attitudes toward tests; if the client can honestly express how he feels toward tests, he will be more likely to listen carefully to the test interpretation given later.

Ivey (1970) has explored the concept of sharing behavior, an analog of attending behavior in which the trainee's attention is focused on himself. Thus, the trainee focuses on his own bodily posture and gestures, maintains eye contact, but psychologically is "inside" himself rather than attending to others and bears the responsibility of carrying on conversation on a single topic. Microtraining procedures have been developed and tested in a preliminary fashion, and early evidence suggests that assisting individuals to express themselves more directly may be a useful skill. However, special adaptions for the interviewing process are still needed.

There are numerous possibilities for training in expression of content. These include a comprehensive set of training materials in test interpretation, diagnostic presentations, information giving in employment service counseling, and balancing expression of information with the client's reaction to that information.

Direct, Mutual Communication

While not originally developed as a microcounseling skill, training in direct, mutual communication may now be considered a relevant skill for counselor and interviewer training, particularly for those interviewers interested in interpersonal openness and directness of expression. Modeled on behaviors taught in sensitivity, encounter, and T-groups, direct, mutual communication is concerned with the interviewer and the interviewee *both* receiving microtraining. If communication is to be mutual, both parties should have the benefit of training. As such, work with interviewers has centered on giving two individuals the opportunity to learn the skill together.

The skill focused on in direct mutual communication was described by Higgins, Ivey, and Uhlemann (1970, p. 21) as follows:

> The skill(s) focused on in this study is one in which two individuals attempt to focus on their interaction as they perceive and feel it, and attempt to share with each other their experience of the other. Rather than talk about politics, their liking of certain movies, books, classes, etc. (the content of most typical conversations), they are to react to the experiences they have (or have had) with each other. They are to share personal feelings with each other and to respond to these shared feelings with new and past reactions to these feelings.

From a psychoanalytic point of view, direct, mutual communication is a frank analysis of the transference relationship occurring between two human beings. Viewed from learning theory, direct, mutual communication is teaching people another way of developing mutual reinforcement modalities with an emphasis on affective comments. Existentially, direct, mutual communication with its emphasis on here and now feelings and experiences may provide interviewers with insight into themselves and the nature of their own existence.

A programmed text (see Appendix A), integrated with videotape models, was developed for direct, mutual communication. A research study examining the effectiveness of the method compared the following three approaches to teaching this skill: (a) full treatment in the traditional microtraining paradigm,

(b) programmed text and video models only with no supervision or video feedback, and (c) reading material only. It was found that the full-treatment group doubled the amount of direct, mutual communication (100% increase); group b increased 50 percent, and group c did not change. While validating the general premise of the study, it seems possible that a completely programmed approach to direct, mutual communication may be feasible and that eventually only a technician or paraprofessional may be required to teach this skill, if under the supervision of a skilled clinician.

An illustration from a typescript of one of the sessions from the full-treatment group may serve to clarify what happens in training in direct, mutual communication. One of the experimental couples was from the Far East and chose to discuss the issue as to whether or not they should return to their homeland.

SESSION 1

Husband: Don't you think that the individual makes a good contribution to his old country when he goes back? Rather than staying here?

Wife: Yes, he would. But then he would not get material gain, he would not get so much money.

Husband: But money is not everything.

Wife: It isn't everything, but it is . . . you want to give the family good educations, good living and everything else, and you can't do this back there.

Husband: But it depends on what we mean by good education, and good living.

(The couple continued this discussion for five minutes with a consistent pattern of "yes, but" with one individual trying to put his point over on the other. Some heat was generated between them. This discussion was basically a confrontation of two opposing points of view.)

SESSION 2

Husband: How do you feel about people staying here in this country and not returning to their native land?

Wife: I personally feel that I would like to stay here, but at the same time I want to return to —————. Of course, I miss my family, but I would like to stay here for some time and make a good living and then take what we need for a good living at home back with us.

Husband: But what about the idea of the "brain drain"? Shouldn't people return to their own country?

Wife: I don't care. Let them stay. If they stay, it is their personal opinion.

Husband: You feel indifferent about it.

Wife: Yes. I don't think we can make others go back to —————, but if they don't, I can't help it. They can stay here.

Husband: I agree with you that this feeling of indifference is quite true. But shouldn't we try to get them to go back? (It may be observed in this session that the couple for the first time made an effort to look at *feelings*. There is the beginning of some listening to one another. However, there is also a tendency to generalize their particular feelings to others rather than looking at their own interaction.)

SESSION 3

Husband: We both seem to have this fear of going back home. I don't think it's really the fear of going back, but a fear of the . . .

Wife: Instability?

Husband: Yes, the fear of instability there, and then the feeling of not having really accomplished to a certain extent what other people have done. And at the same time, this nagging thought comes to my mind always, you have to go back. You have to go back. What do you feel about this fear?

Wife: I feel insecure too. I don't know what will happen if we go back. I really want to go back today to ——————— if we have things, but I am very scared. What will we do? We don't have anything back home.

Husband: Yes, what is your feeling now at this moment? You can think about what we would have and what we would not have. What do you feel about not having it?

Wife: There is just a blank. I see nothing. The future makes me afraid. We have no definite opportunities even in ——————— or here.

Husband: It makes me feel right now that I'm not capable of doing it. How does my inability make you feel?

Wife: I feel sorry. And I want you to do something about it. Keep trying and somehow we will manage it. If you can't, we both can do something.

(The couple went on to constructive discussion of the problem at hand, more fully aware of the issues underlying this complex decision. It may be observed in this third session that the couple was able to share feelings and attitudes of fear and, at the same time, to listen constructively to one another. An increased emphasis on feelings may be observed. Feelings, however, are viewed in a context of life and are used positively to establish a closer relationship and make a more sound decision. (Higgins, Ivey, and Uhlemann (1970, p. 24).)

Direct, mutual communication has been used in counselor and therapist training with some dramatic results. Therapists who have a special interest in encounter groups or existential psychology may find that the often highly charged, dramatic methods of this microtraining skill may prove helpful in making their concepts more explicit. The methods of direct, mutual communication also provide a laboratory in which the behavioral aspects of interpersonal openness may be systematically explored.

For the interviewer in training, experience in direct, mutual communication may aid in confronting a passive or hostile client with his own present perceptions. The video models and accompanying materials serve as a model of honesty and directness; after viewing them, the novice may begin to realize that he himself may be the most important dimension in the counseling and interviewing process.

INTERPRETATION

Interpretation involves both attending and self-expression and is a broader skill than any discussed thus far. The successful interviewer must be able both to listen to his client and to express himself so that the client understands him. The skill of interpretation was developed by Moreland and Ivey (1969) and has proven to be the most challenging and complex skill within the microcounseling paradigm. Conceptually, interpretation is based on an adaption of Levy's stimulating work, *Psychological Interpretation* (1963). Levy has said, "To sum up, psychological interpretation, viewed as a behavior . . . consists of bringing an alternate frame of reference, or language system, to bear upon a set of observations or behaviors, with the end in view of making them more amenable to manipulation" (p. 7).

While interpretations may vary in content, depending upon the theoretical orientation from which they are drawn, they all have a common element. When an interviewer makes an interpretation, he is presenting the client with a new frame of reference through which the client can view his problem and hopefully, better understand and deal with it. Seen in this light, an interpretation is not unlike either a paraphrase or a reflection of feeling. However, the new frame of reference is also tied to the interviewer's perception of the situation. As such, self-expression skills become especially important.

One function of both the paraphrase and the reflection of feeling is to crystallize for the client either the objective content or the feeling components of what has just been said. In paraphrasing and reflection of feeling, the interviewer remains, for the most part, within the client's *own* frame of reference. However, in interpretation, the interviewer provides the client with a *new*, potentially more functional frame of reference.

The locus and time frame of interviewer attention has changed. While the interviewer still attends to the client in the "here and now," he is also attending to past client comments and to his personal theoretical orientation. When giving an interpretation to the client, the counselor has many alternatives at a variety of levels of depth available to him. He can interpret the comment primarily from the client's point of view, in which case his interpretation will appear similar to a paraphrase or reflection of feeling; he can make an interpretation from his own theoretical point of view restating the client's comments in a totally new frame of reference. More likely, the interpretation will contain elements of both the client's and the interviewer's perceptions.

Moreland and Ivey (1969, p. 1) made the following comment on the depth of interpretation:

> Interpretation has traditionally been viewed as mystical activity in which the interviewer reaches into the depths of the client's personality and provides him with new insight. However, when one conceives of an interpretation as merely a new frame of reference, the concept of depth takes on a much less formidable aura. Viewed in this light, the depth of a given interpretation refers to the magnitude of the discrepancy between the frame of reference from which the client is operating and the frame of reference supplied by the interviewer. For example, a client may report a dream in which a seedling he had planted grew into a tree and was mysteriously cut down. The interviewer could make a number of interpretations which vary in terms of their depth.
> 1. You lost something you really cared about.
> 2. Your life has had a number of disappointments.
> 3. You're very unsure of your successes.
> 4. You're afraid of losing your penis.

The value of a feeling reflection or a paraphrase is gauged by the client's verbal or nonverbal reaction to it. One criterion for the value of a single interpretation is whether or not the client can utilize it to cope more effectively with his problem, *both* intellectually and emotionally. In the above examples, any of the interpretations could be facilitating or nonfacilitating, depending on the reaction of the client. In the early stages of therapy, the client may be able to utilize the first example, while later he may understand and use the more complex depth interpretations. Another criterion for the validity of the interpretation is the interviewer's personal comfort with his view of the client's world. If the interviewer is not congruent with himself and the client, the interpretation is less likely to be accepted.

An interpretation is, by definition, a semantic integration of cognitive and affective states. Interpretation does not emphasize feelings as distinct from interview verbal content but attempts to present the essence of the individual as seen from another vantage point. The skilled therapist should have at hand a variety of interpretations of differing depth levels concerning his client's behavior.

In microtraining, interpretation is taught as a general skill rather than as one associated with a particular theoretical discipline. Thus trainees are encouraged to free themselves and give a variety of alternative interpretations to the same behavior in practice situations. In microtraining sessions, a role played client gives a standard stimulus to which the interviewer can respond with a variety of interpretations and note their effectiveness.

Interpretation also has validity in interviewing situations which are not necessarily therapeutic. The employment interviewer may believe he is talking with a malingerer. He notes several comments, threaded throughout the session, suggestive of a person who is not telling the truth. When the interviewer sums up these separate but related comments, adds his own evaluation of them, and allows the individual to rethink these ideas, he is engaging in an interpretation. Like the therapist, his interpretation is most effective when he is comfortable with his perception and feels his client can use the interpretation to explore the issue in more depth. It may be seen that the interviewer has taken an *ad hoc* theoretical framework developed from his own experience, integrated it with data from the interviewee's conversation and behavior, and provided the interviewee with an interpretation of the situation in the hope that further discussion of the issue will occur.

In summary, interpretation can be said to involve several distinct attentional frameworks. First, the interviewer attends to and reinforces a variety of client comments through paraphrasing and reflection. Simultaneously, the interviewer is relating data provided by the client to past information and his own theoretical framework. When the interviewer makes an interpretation, he summarizes his observations in a frame of reference which gives the client a new way of viewing himself or the situation. Finally, once having made an interpretation, the counselor should be able to attend to the client's verbal and nonverbal reactions and revise his interpretation as appropriate.

At this point, it appears useful to discuss some characteristics which distinguish interpretation from paraphrasing and reflection of feeling.

> *Client* (who has had a record of absenteeism): I really feel badly about missing so much work.

> *Interviewer*: You're really troubled and worried. (Reflection of feeling.)
> You've been missing a lot of work. (Paraphrase.)
> You've missed a lot of work and you are aware of how the company views absenteeism. This gives you concern as to where you stand. (Interpretation.)

Reflection of feeling takes data from the client and focuses on emotional aspects. The paraphrase focuses on the content of the problem. Interpretation attends to both emotional and objective components; in addition, the interviewer's observations and frame of reference are added.

Another example from psychotherapy is as follows:

> *Client* (with agitation): My wife and I had a fight last night after watching a sexually exciting movie. I tried to make love and she rejected me again.
> *Counselor*: You're upset about and troubled about what happened. (Reflection of feeling.)
> Your fight followed a sexually exciting movie. (Paraphrase.)
> The movie stimulated you sexually and you sought to make love, expecting your wife to reject you once again. (Interpretation.)
> You've mentioned several times that you are interested in making love with your wife after some external sexual stimulation. You've never mentioned your wife as being sexually exciting. (Interpretation.)
> The feelings of rejection trouble you. Are these feelings similar to some feelings you mentioned in the dream last week? (Interpretation.)
> As I see you here and now, you seem very upset. Your hand is clenched. You'd like to do something right now but you don't know what. (Interpretation.)

In each example of interpretation, the interviewer takes a part of the essence of what the client has said (both emotionally and intellectually) and summarizes it for him, adding other data which he considers relevant. A multitude of interpretations are possible with any client utterance and will vary with the theoretical orientation of the interviewer.

Psychological interpretations demand important skills on the part of the interviewer. Microtraining techniques will not develop fully skilled interpreters, but defining more precisely the nature of the interpretative process should help the beginning counselor and interviewer.

INTEGRATING SEVERAL SKILLS IN ONE TRAINING SESSION

Once a counselor-in-training has demonstrated the ability to engage in the specific skills of interviewing, he needs assistance in integrating skills into longer practice interviewing sessions. Several possibilities have been explored and have shown promise as methods to assist the individual bridge the gap between theory and practice in interviewing.

One model which has been successfully employed is half-hour sessions in which a real or role-played client meets with the trainee for an open-ended session. The trainee is simply instructed to interview the client as the situation demands. Following the session, the videotape is reviewed and trainee interviewing leads are compared with specific microtraining models. This method is closely related to much of present interviewing training, except that the trainee's interviewing behavior may be tested against previously defined skills of interviewing. Supervision thus becomes more precise and potentially profitable to the trainee.

A major alternative involves combining the above approach with the Interpersonal Process Recall (IPR) methods of Kagan and Krathwohl (1967). In this setting, the client is brought into the viewing session and asked to give his reactions and feelings toward the trainee's interviewing style. Not only does this approach help the trainee grow, but it also provides an additional interviewing tool as well, for many trainees express themselves more openly in the second session than the first.

A third model is provided by the Miller, Morrill, Uhlemann (1970) study discussed in the preceding section. Here a specific problem area is defined. It may be test interpretation, giving a client information about the company, or a particular emotional problem discussed by a role-played client. In this model, the counselor has a specific problem area defined and is required to use several skills. This model allows for the presentation of expert models of performance against which the trainee may compare himself.

A variety of other alternatives for teaching integrative interviewing skills are possible. Shorter sessions of ten to fifteen minutes, where combinations of two or three skills are employed alternatively, have proven profitable. In one model, trainees alternatively reinforce emotional and cognitive comments of the client, thus demonstrating their ability to direct the content of the interview. Other microtraining sessions might focus on beginning and ending the counseling session.

SUMMARY

The microtraining framework provides a general system for teaching virtually any counseling or interviewing skill. The skills presented illustrate the possibilities for introducing novice interviewers to the complex processes of human interaction. Microtraining is not aligned with a specific theory; it is a general training model adaptable to a variety of theoretical orientations.

It is possible to develop advanced skills for highly trained therapists who may be interested in learning new ideas and methods. At another level, it is equally feasible to develop skills which can be taught to individuals who serve as counselor aides or paraprofessionals. Microtraining is most effective when adapted to meet the needs of the individuals concerned and is only meaningful when it meets both the trainer and trainees' needs.

Attending behavior is related to many of the skills proposed in this chapter. In the general area of listening skills, the trainee attends to others, in self-expression skills he attends to himself, while interpretation demands that he do both simultaneously. For some, the constructs of attending behavior and attention may seem simplistic and unnecessary; others may find them useful as they relate microtraining to their unique situations.

Chapter Five

USING MICROTRAINING AS A
TEACHING TOOL

M ICROTRAINING AND MICROCOUNSELING represent an open
system, an approach to interviewing training which allows for
alternatives and variations. We have found that changing and
adapting the basic framework to meet the needs of the individual
being trained, his supervisor, and the setting in which they work
results in the most effective and enjoyable learning experience.

Thus, this chapter has a dual purpose, (a) to present specific
suggestions for effecting and launching a microcounseling program and (b) to summarize major alternatives to be considered
in adapting this framework to varying settings.

TEACHING MICROCOUNSELING SKILLS TO INDIVIDUALS

There is a very real danger that the teaching of microcounseling skills can become mechanical and fixed. After one
has learned the procedures and enjoyed the first flush of success,
it is possible to develop a routine in which the supervisor loses
his personal involvement with the trainees. When this happens,
we have often observed that the trainees learn the skills which
are being taught but are not enthused by the procedures and
have trouble generalizing newly learned behaviors to the actual
counseling setting.

We have learned that teaching the specific skills of counseling
involves important supervisory-counseling skills. As noted earlier,
the supervisor must model the skills he is teaching. For example,
it is possible to teach attending behavior to a trainee and fail to
attend to the trainee's questions and possible resistance toward
the entire procedure. The supervisor in such situations must
listen to the trainee and observe his needs at the moment. A
trainee may be concerned over the cosmetic effect of seeing

himself on television for the first time. The supervisor can facilitate learning by helping the trainee talk out his feelings. A trainee may feel that he is not capable of engaging in the behavior being taught. At such points, superior counseling and supervisory skills are essential if trainee growth through micro-training is to occur.

With some trainees, supplementing the regular program with role playing is most helpful. Occasionally, a modern Rogerian approach is useful. The supervisor might say to the trainee, "I have the feeling right now that you are nervous about the training." Such leads can help the trainee explore himself and his attitudes. However, it is essential that the supervisor not simply role-play reflection of feeling; such behavior is most effective when the supervisor really cares about his trainee and seeks to develop a more mutual relationship with him. This live-modeling approach adds to the genuineness of the encounter.

It might be useful to illustrate in more detail the way in which relationship skills are important in teaching a single skill. When teaching attending behavior, the entire session is begun in a casual and friendly (but organized) fashion. Trainees are welcomed and invited to inspect the television recording facility. Questions regarding the experience are often raised and much can be done at this stage to alleviate anxiety.

After the initial five-minute videotaping session, the first task of the supervisor is to establish a more genuine relationship with the trainee. This may be done by a variety of means, but basically the supervisor must attend to the client and respond to his immediate needs, even if this means delaying the training procedures. Generally speaking, the question "How did it go?" or "How do you feel?" provides sufficient material for the sensitive trainer to determine how best to establish a relationship with that particular individual. With nervous trainees, we have occasionally instituted informal instruction in systematic relaxation. Most trainees, however, are relatively relaxed and eager to move forward with the instructional procedures.

Throughout the supervisory session, we provide opportunities for the trainee to interact with us in any way he chooses. If he seems resistant, we may use this resistance as a leverage to obtain a relationship with him. Trainees are encouraged to examine the meaningfulness of the skill which we are teaching. However, when confronted with a good deal of talk or resistance on the part of the trainee, we sometimes suggest a short-term contract in which the trainee agrees to try on the skill during this session and we will talk with him at greater length later. We suggest that "This is simply one view of counseling. All we are asking you to do is 'try on' some new and specific behavior. If you like it, you may continue it. If not, feel free to forget it. Unless the behavior fits and feels natural, it will be of no use to you." This "if you listen to me, I'll listen to you" contract has proven most fruitful and has resulted in subsequent changes or additions to our basic training procedures.

When viewing the modeling tape or reviewing the five-minute tape made by the trainee, it is usually helpful to stop the tape and give the trainee an opportunity to react—or you may wish to give specific reactions of your own. However, it is vital that the trainee not be overwhelmed by data. Sometimes too many behaviors are taught at once or a specific skill is described in too minute detail. Microtraining procedures are not concerned with producing effective counselors in one session. The primary concern is helping trainees to grow with time. As such, it is preferable that most trainees be given one to three specific suggestions as to how they might improve. Otherwise, the suggestions are forgotten and a trainee is made more tense.

Basically, all we ask of our trainees is some improvement from their starting point. While most reach criterion levels rather quickly, others require several sessions. Some trainees are better in their first five-minute session than others are after several training units. Our approach has always been to reward improvement and not to judge the level of effectiveness. We find that this approach usually brings even the most "unpromising" trainee to satisfactory performance. As such, microtraining is a highly individualized process.

In summary, the above points center on the counseling and supervisory skills of the trainer. If he- is able to establish a unique and meaningful relationship with the trainee, improvement in both immediate and future performance seems almost inevitable. If the supervisor finds himself becoming bored or losing effectiveness with the process despite these suggestions, it may be wise to ask another individual with similar supervisory skills to serve as a replacement. A procedure such as micro-counseling requires personal involvement if it is to succeed, and like all things, one eventually finds a need for change.

Microcounseling is well-defined procedurally so that relatively untrained individuals such as paraprofessionals or students can be utilized as trainers. In such settings, the counseling or personnel supervisor becomes a roving consultant, assisting his staff to actually run the training program. A basic model to train paraprofessionals has been explored by Haase and DiMattia (1970). A major suggestion for the utilization of paraprofessionals in training of others is that adequate training in supervisory skills be added to basic training in the microcounseling model.

DEVELOPING MICROTRAINING MATERIALS AND VIDEO MODELING TAPES

When one develops materials for microcounseling, he finds that he learns more about the skills than do those he will eventually teach. Much thought and care must go into developing written or programmed materials which communicate the underlying concepts of a basic skill. Similarly, developing a video or film sequence to illustrate the behavior in question is a demanding task. However, with some basic guidelines, the task is pleasant and an important learning experience for the person who develops the materials.

As such, a possibility which one may wish to consider in materials development is simply giving students the problem of defining the skills of interviewing in behavioral terms. With some guidance from the trainer, this can be a successful method of teaching basic skills. This approach, however, takes a good deal of time and equipment and perhaps should be reserved for advanced trainees who may go into counseling or personnel supervision.

The first step in developing materials for microtraining is

the selection of the skill or specific behavior. If the skill is defined as attending behavior, a good way to begin is to place models of poor attention on videotape, for it is relatively easy to model ineffective interviewing. Once one views the ineffective model, it becomes possible to identify the specific behaviors which comprise effective demonstration of the behavior in question. Individuals who model ineffective listening on videotape typically avoid eye contact, show physical discomfort, and engage in topic jumping and interruption. Viewing these negative behaviors, then, makes it possible to develop positive models representing an antithesis.

If the behavior to be developed was focused on positive responses to a negative employee, the first model might have the interviewer alternatively ignoring and interrupting the employee, thus demonstrating a generally ineffective confronting approach (the word "generally" is inserted, as we have found that virtually any behavior is appropriate in some situation). The positive model then might consist of attending behavior plus certain expressive skills such as direct, mutual communication and giving factual information to the employee. Through this method, new skill tapes using the basic concepts of microtraining can be adapted to many situations.

Having identified general positive and negative models of the behavior in question, it is then feasible to establish more complete working models of the behavior. As an example of a modeling tape, attending behavior consists of a one-minute segment without sound, illustrating positive attention on the part of the interviewer. (During this segment, the trainer talks with the trainee about the importance of nonverbal communication and points out eye contact and physical posture patterns.) This is followed by a minute of a soundless negative model with poor eye-contact patterns and a closed or tight physical posture. Next the sound comes on and a minute of poor verbal following behavior is shown in which the interviewer topic jumps, talks about himself, and interrupts. A final two-to-three minute segment consists of the counselor engaging in positive attending behavior both verbally and nonverbally.

The reflection-of-feeling modeling tapes, typically five to

seven minutes in length, consist of three examples, one negative and two positive. The negative model focuses on objective content and ignores obvious feelings on the part of the client. The positive models demonstrate emotional responses to the client's utterances.

The summarization-of-feeling modeling tape has varied in length from five to ten minutes. In this model, a client discusses a problem with the counselor who uses attending behavior and reflection of feeling. At crucial points, the counselor summarizes the client's emotions over the session to that point. Two summarizations are positive, two negative.

The nature of the direct, mutual communication modeling tape is most apparent from the programmed text in the appendix. In this case, written programmed materials were integrated with video models illustrating specific aspects of open communication among pairs of individuals. We have found that those who have worked in T-groups or sensitivity training are best at providing models of direct, mutual communication.

It can be seen that modeling tapes for each skill have tended to take a slightly different form. Those who have utilized microcounseling in their training programs have consistently adapted the modeling tapes and skills to suit their own particular needs and theoretical persuasions. We do not particularly commend the above approaches to video modeling tapes, but have found them effective in our setting.

Once a video modeling tape has been developed, it is possible to develop a written manual. Samples of manuals are available in the appendix. Each manual has gone through several revisions in an attempt to make the concept more specific to the population being taught. When teaching attending behavior to children, for example, a simple statement of about a paragraph in length seems appropriate. When working with advanced clinical graduate students, more sophisticated and theoretically oriented statements may be useful.

CLIENTS IN THE MICROTRAINING PROCESS

It is the client who provides the life and rationale for

microcounseling and microtraining processes. Designed as a bridge between classroom theories of counseling and interviewing and actual practice in the field, microtraining provides maximum realism with a minimum of danger to clients and/or prospective counselors.

A major question in the early stages of research in microcounseling centered on how real the five-minute sessions would be. Would paid and volunteer clients be representative of those whom counselors might interview at later points or would these be artificial and contrived sessions? Clinical observation by numerous individuals has revealed that the sessions are indeed real; clients talk about real issues and concerns, and except for the length of the sessions, very real parallels to actual counseling exist.

Clients appear to enjoy and appreciate the opportunity to participate in microcounseling training sessions, willingly cooperate with filling out evaluation forms, and usually volunteer to return for more sessions. On many occasions when we have paid clients to serve as research subjects, we have found them saying they benefited from the sessions and therefore do not wish to accept payment. To date, observation and follow-up of clients have not found any individuals who feel negatively toward the process. Nonetheless, it seems desirable to have fully trained professional counselors or supervisors on hand to supervise the work of a microcounseling clinic.

When volunteer clients are not readily available, role playing between pairs of counseling or interviewing trainees has proven effective. In role-played sessions, we have found that the situation becomes surprisingly real, and preliminary evidence suggests that this approach to microtraining may be as effective as more usual methods. As experimentation with role playing has continued, we have found that many pairs of trainees prefer to talk about real concerns rather than taking someone else's role. Needless to say, sessions of this nature become concerned with problems of real depth, and this method of training requires careful supervision by experienced staff. The potential for personal and professional growth, however, is important in such sessions and can be followed up by counseling, referral, or group sessions.

With advanced trainees, Kagan and Krathwohl's Interpersonal Process Recall (1967) methods have proven most effective. Clients remain in the microtraining session and discuss their reactions with the trainee and his supervisor. This immediate and direct feedback from the client's world has proven most helpful in promoting trainee growth. Trainees are often more able to listen to their clients than their supervisors.

Finally, it should be observed that microtraining procedures in the "skill of being a client" may be useful. Truax's vicarious therapy (1965, 1966) has demonstrated the validity of pretraining a client prior to counseling sessions. Clients who have been taught skills to use in counseling sessions tend to view counseling more positively and benefit more from sessions. Haase, Forsyth, Julius, and Lee (1969) have applied the microtraining framework to college counseling center clients and found that client pre-training facilitated subsequent interviews. Although micro-counseling procedures were not used, a closely parallel study by Whalen (1969) demonstrated that video modeling films could facilitate group-encounter processes.

While the preceding examples have focused on counseling and therapy, useful analogies can be drawn to personnel or employment interviewing. It appears that volunteer clients from work settings will perform successfully as microtraining clients. However, evaluation may concern employees as much or more than students in a course. Some may fear that promotions or raises depend on their performance. Under such conditions, role-played sessions may be preferable. Skillful, honest supervision seems essential, because such fears can only damage the effectiveness of the microtraining sessions.

Realness is important to microtraining. If sessions seem artificial, awkward, or stereotyped, the supervisor will want to look at his *relationship* with his trainees and clients. Any procedure which is as clearly defined as microtraining has the danger of becoming stereotyped and losing touch with original goals. Our experience suggests that failures in microcounseling are often failures of the supervisor to relate with his trainees and volunteer clients on a personal basis.

VIDEO EQUIPMENT

The basic dimensions of focusing on a single skill of interviewing, feedback, supervision and practice can be accomplished without video equipment. However, videotape and the resulting pictorial and sound feedback is an impressively powerful tool.

Foremost in value is *feedback* from interviewing sessions. The trainee has the opportunity to view himself in action, and there can be no dispute about what happened in a session when it appears on videotape. The trainee can see what he likes about himself and what he might like to change. Simultaneously, the trainee has the opportunity to *view video models* of other interviewers demonstrating the specific skill. Bandura and Walters (1963) have conclusively demonstrated the importance of modeling in human learning processes. Trainees learn new interviewing skills more quickly and easily when they see skills demonstrated by experts.

Many trainees are nervous about their first sessions in front of a video camera and some special attention may have to be paid to a cosmetic effect of concern over physical appearance during the first microtraining session. However, if a positive and supportive supervisor is present, video anxieties appear to dissipate. It is particularly helpful if primarily positive aspects of the first five-minute session are stressed. Trainees are anxious to learn the skills and are quite capable of pointing out where they failed to engage in the skill being taught.

Stoller (1965) has pointed out the importance of "focused feedback" in therapeutic work with videotape. Focused feedback means that the supervisor focuses training only on a single dimension of the trainee's behavior and does not try to remake the trainee all at once. When one sees a trainee committing six or seven errors in the course of a five-minute session, it is tempting to try to rearrange the trainee's total performance for the next session. We have found it preferable to say to the trainee, "We do not expect you to produce a perfect interview, we only want to see improvement in this one area." Not only does this reassure the trainee, but he is also gratified to see improvement in the specific area, whereas if all skills were stressed at once, improvement might be painfully slow. Interestingly, we have also found that stressing a single skill and omitting reference to other problems often results in improvement in other areas which have been ignored. Even though microtraining divides counseling into specific dimensions, these dimensions are related, and improvement in one area brings improvement in others as well.

Videotape equipment has been blessed with improved reliability and simplicity in recent years. Systems only slightly more complex than audiotape recorders now exist. In one recent study, we used junior high school students as videotape operators. Videotape cassettes, streamlined portable recorders and cameras, and compatible systems between competing companies all facilitate videotape use. Equipment costs have been reduced dramatically in recent years and can be expected to be further lowered.

Two models of equipment use can be identified. One is represented by studio-type operations in which videotape equipment is centrally located with quality light and sound systems, technicians, and supporting services all available. While the reliability of equipment is improved under such systems, it has been found that use of equipment diminishes. We favor a less complicated and less expensive model of equipment usage. Videotape systems are sufficiently reliable and durable that they can be used on a take-out basis much as audiotape recorders or film systems in any school. Experience has proven that microtraining can be successful in a studio-type environment with a concealed camera (which, of course, has been shown to the trainee and client prior to the session) or with the supervisor running portable equipment in the same room as the trainee and his client.

Individuals must find their own way to use video equipment. There are many models of video laboratories that can be developed with split screens, special effect generators, and other useful techniques. Such special equipment may be most helpful in research settings which require detailed examination of specific dimensions. For general use, however, inexpensive, portable equipment will prove satisfactory. In effect, all that is needed for microtraining with video equipment is the equipment, a trainee, a client, a supervisor, and a room. The less complicated the operation, the more likely that the equipment will be used extensively.

ALTERNATIVE MICROTRAINING MODELS

The original microcounseling model has been outlined in Chapter 1. There are, however, a multitude of other models, which can include the basic dimensions of focusing on a specific skill, provision of a written or programmed manual, demonstration via modeling of the skill to be taught, and reward of appropriate trainee behavior.

Group models of training have proven most effective. For example, six to eight trainees may be taught attending behavior together. They are paired for the first five-minute sessions and are each videorecorded. All trainees then receive instruction via a manual, view a modeling tape, and finally criticize their tapes as a group. The final five-minute sessions are again videorecorded and observed. The total time elapsed is approximately two hours.

Original microtraining sessions had trainees attempt positive behaviors in the first five-minute sessions. While this has been effective, recent experimentation has suggested that having trainees deliberately demonstrate negative behavior in the first five-minute session results in better learning of skills. In demonstrating what reflection of feeling or attending behavior is not, trainees more readily grasp the skill. Teaching by contrast has become a standard part of microtraining procedures. This approach has been helpful to those trainees who are concerned and anxious over their television appearance. When a person demonstrates negative behavior in the first session, improvement in the second session is certain. This, in turn, seems to free the individual for later growth.

Audiotape may be substituted for videotape but has a danger of focusing on words alone and missing the vital nonverbal dimensions of the encounter. However, if used in a group situation or with skilled supervision, feedback on trainee performance is still available. Models of the skill may be demonstrated or role played by the supervisor.

Most individuals will learn attending behavior skills within a one-hour cycle of counsel-recounsel. Complex skills such as reflection of feeling, summarization, and interpretation require two cycles of from ninety minutes to two hours. For those who do not learn the behaviors within a two-hour period, recycling for another session is recommended. Most trainees learn the specific skills when sufficient recycling is permitted.

The five-minute session for microtraining is an arbitrary figure. Some have criticized this length as insufficient for any real counseling to occur. Observation, however, reveals that five minutes is a substantial period for most skills. Time variations of from three to ten minutes have been explored, with satisfactory results. More complex skills such as interpretation and summarization seem to require a longer period of time. Basically, the length of the session depends on the skill, the individual, and the supervisor.

Special modifications in the microcounseling skill may be necessary for some trainees. For example, when teaching attending behavior to younger children or especially anxious individuals, three dimensions of eye contact, verbal and physical attention may be more than is possible to learn at one sitting. In such a case, it is recommended that the single skill of eye contact be taught, then nonverbal attention, and finally verbal following patterns. These skills may be integrated into attending behavior at a later point. Justifying the approach is the work of Polanyi (1966) on tacit knowing cited earlier. As one learns a specific skill, it eventually becomes habituated and integrated into a larger whole, allowing the individual to move to higher levels of growth and expression. Koestler (1964) also describes the same phenomenon.

An effective group program in counseling skills has been used in some classrooms. Students who have been introduced at a prior time to the basic microtraining framework are advised that they are to identify a specific skill of counseling. They select their own skill and develop their own modeling tapes and written materials.

Even sharper breaks with the basic microcounseling model are possible. Telling individuals about the skill and demonstrating it in a brief role-playing situation sometimes proves sufficient for the skill to be learned and generalized. Microcounseling skills can be and have been taught with the first five-minute session eliminated, omission of modeling tapes, with or without a supervisor, and with changes in order of presentation of materials. Further, informal observation suggests that skills are taught most effectively when the supervisor changes the model to suit his own preferences and needs. People seem to need to own what they are doing, and adaptation of the basic model tends to produce more involvement. Microtraining is sufficiently flexible that an almost infinite number of changes are possible. What does seem important, however, is that the four basic dimensions of single skills, feedback, models, and supervision are included in some form.

ETHICAL CONSIDERATIONS

We have found that microcounseling and its videotape methods are useful tools for training. While teaching the direct, mutual communication skill, we have found trainees expressing themselves openly and freely. Further, a volunteer or paid client may sometimes open himself to an important problem area in his life. In short, we are dealing with *people* and with a powerful method of effecting human change.

The confidence of microtraining clients must be kept. It is not permissible to show videotapes of training sessions without the client's (and trainee's) signed permission. Even if permission is granted, professional ethics demand careful consideration of what types of materials are presented to what types of groups outside of the training sessions.

For the occasional volunteer client who discusses a problem which requires further counseling or follow-up, a professional staff supervisor should be available throughout microtraining sessions. If microtraining sessions are run by advanced graduate students or paraprofessionals, regular supervision and examination of their work is essential.

The trainee's rights must also be protected. He is entitled to the same professional and personal respect that is accorded to microtraining clients. Trainees, when role-playing clients or developing skills focusing on sharing their own feelings, may show themselves in need of further counseling. Follow-up counseling and referral services should be available.

Both trainees and clients should be fully aware of videotape equipment. All our trainees and clients are shown video equipment before they began their sessions. While it has not happened to date, if a client or trainee decides against videotaping, the session should proceed with the camera turned off. At a later date when the trainee or client is more secure, videotaping can proceed.

Finally, microtraining is neither a panacea nor a cure-all. It is simply a new and promising method of interviewing training. Further research to determine parameters of effectiveness and generalization is needed. The training procedures of microcounseling should not be seen as equipping an individual to be fully effective as a counselor but as a bridge between theoretical methodology and actual practice. Much more goes into producing an effective counselor or interviewer than microtraining techniques alone.

Chapter Six

MICROTRAINING AS USED IN
OTHER SETTINGS

$\mathbf{M}$ ICROCOUNSELING AND MICROTRAINING have many applications beyind the dyadic interview. The concepts of single skill emphasis, presentation of models, feedback, and positive supervision have implications for use in various fields other than counseling. This chapter summarizes related, innovative uses of microtraining techniques in other settings.

TEACHER TRAINING

Microcounseling was originally based on the microteaching format developed at Stanford University by Allen (1967), Aubertine (1967), and their colleagues. The microteaching framework is basically identical to microtraining with a few modifications. Foremost among these is that the teacher instructs a small group of students (usually four or five) for a brief period of time ranging from five to twenty-five minutes. The teacher's lesson is designed as a small, self-contained unit, whereas in microcounseling, the sessions tend to be open-ended and terminated at a fixed point in time by the supervisor.

A formal "package" of film models of microteaching skills is now sold commercially. When film models are used in connection with microteaching, additional equipment is required. Allen, Ryan, Bush, and Cooper (1969) have developed eighteen microteaching skills and organized them into the following four "skill clusters":

1. Response repertoire
   a. Verbal responses
   b. Nonverbal responses

    c. Verbal and nonverbal responses
2. Questioning skills
    a. Fluency in asking questions
    b. Probing questions
    c. Higher order questions
    d. Divergent questions
3. Creating student involvement
    a. Set induction
    b. Stimulus variation
    c. Closure
4. Increasing student participation
    a. Reinforcement
    b. Recognizing attending behavior
    c. Silence and nonverbal cues
    d. Cueing
5. Presentation skills
    a. Completeness of communication
    b. Lecturing
    c. Use of examples
    d. Planned repetition

This extensive list of skills has evolved from an *ad hoc* atheoretical base. The prime determinant of a skill's inclusion was dependent on whether or not the skill was identifiable, measurable, and relevant to the teaching process. Allen and his colleagues view microteaching as an open system permitting the modification of existing skills or the identification and addition of new skills.

Several of the skills developed through microteaching have direct application in interviewing. The skill of reinforcement, for example, assists teachers to correct random, indiscriminate reinforcement of pupil responses and to use reinforcement in a more positive fashion. Silence and nonverbal communication is a particularly dramatic microteaching skill. For example, a teacher in a film model asks a small group of children a single question and then keeps the group moving smoothly for five minutes without saying a word, through the use of a wide variety of gestures and expressions.

Microteaching skills tend to focus on control of students and imparting information. It would seem that the use of some microcounseling skills might assist teachers in listening more effectively to children, particularly if education is viewed as a two-way process. Similarly, counselors and interviewers may be well advised to consider the presentation and communication skills of microteaching as a supplement for influencing clients in a positive direction.

The literature on microteaching is becoming extensive, and research efforts to date suggest that microteaching techniques facilitate learning and make teacher education less ambiguous. Flanders (in Allen and Ryan, 1969) reports that half of American teacher education institutions utilize some form of microteaching. Perlberg and Bryant (1968) have introduced microteaching into the college setting in group and individual models. More recently, Perlberg, Peri, and Weinreb (1970) have extended the microteaching model to the training of dental educators at Tel Aviv University in Israel.

USING MICROTRAINING TO TEACH BEHAVIORAL SKILLS

Ivey and Rollin (in press) are currently exploring the degree to which training in human relations behaviors can expand the range of alternatives available to an individual. If microteaching is effective in teacher training and proves useful in counselor and interviewer training, a similar framework can be used to teach individuals the developmental skills of living or the skills of being people.

Ivey and Rollin are instructing college students in specific behavioral skills (e.g. relaxation, attending behavior, nonverbal skills, decision making, self-expression skills) and have found the microtraining framework a useful method of teaching interpersonal skills. The primary area for training thus far has been attending behavior and Rollin (1970) has demonstrated that it is possible to teach this skill to students who are not interviewers or counselor trainees.

The "do-use-teach" model is important in the behavioral-skills curriculum. Participants are first asked to demonstrate their ability to engage in, for example, attending behavior as taught in the microtraining framework. However, demonstration of the ability to engage in a behavioral skill is insufficient in itself and raises a major question, "How can the behavioral skill be transferred to daily life?" In many group programs, little effort has been spent to show participants how they can transfer newly learned behaviors and ideas to their daily life. In the use portion of the behavioral-objectives training program, each participant makes a contract with the trainer to use attending behavior in his daily life. Some trainees practice attending and nonattending behaviors with their families, others do so in business or group situations. This commitment to direct practice ensures learning of a skill and increases retention.

Even though a person can demonstrate and use a behavioral skill such as attending behavior, this still does not indicate full knowledge of what has been learned. A motto of the behavioral objectives group at the University of Massachusetts is, "You don't understand what you have learned until you can teach it to someone else." As a final step, the trainee must demonstrate his ability to teach some aspect of attending behavior to others. Trainees have taught attending behavior to children, family, and friends using many innovative methods and concepts which the project staff have in turn used to enrich and enliven their own teaching.

The behavioral objectives curriculum in human relations training has been adopted as a regular portion of the teacher training program at the University of Massachusetts. Additional skills are currently being developed to facilitate individual communication and relationships with others. Eventually, a human relations laboratory-library is anticipated, wherein students may be oriented to the skills content of the program and self-select those skills appropriate to their own needs. While it has not yet been possible to implement the concepts of skill self-selection, the involvement of individuals in selecting their own areas for behavioral change may prove an important and facilitating method for increasing individual personal growth.

TEACHING STUDENTS SKILLS OF BEING STUDENTS

Ivey and Hinkle (1970) describe the results of teaching college students attending behavior. A group of six students was taught attending behavior and returned to their seminar in a psychology course, which was then videotaped. The students began class participation with typical student behavior of note-taking and passive listening. The professor lectured, unaware of any prearranged plan. His presentation was factual and detailed, but he was completely note-centered, paid no attention to the students, used no gestures, and spoke in a monotone. After a time, on a prearranged signal, the students began deliberate attending behavior through attentive posture and eye contact. Within thirty seconds, the professor gestured for the first time, his verbal rate increased, and a lively session ensued. Following another signal, the class stopped attending. Within ninety seconds, the professor, after some painful seeking for continued reinforcement, returned to his notes and resumed the same deliberate lecture posture described at the first of the presentation.

The professor was completely unaware of the impact the class was having on him. He later noted their interest in the middle of his presentation and commented that "sometimes you hit material that interests them." Upon viewing the tape, he realized he could have worked more effectively with the class by responding to them more directly. Discussion with the students following the experiment revealed the following: (a) it was difficult to start paying attention to the professor, as they had established a prior pattern of minimal involvement in the seminar, (b) once the professor unconsciously noted their attending behavior and became more involved with them, the students found themselves lost in his presentation and their feigned attending became real attention, (c) upon the signal to stop attending, the students found it difficult to change set, for they realized that their involvement in the instructional process was an important one.

An eighth-grade girl viewing the videotape at a demonstration commented, "Now I know what I have been doing. I have this awful math teacher who is so dull. But I asked for a seat in front of the room and I tried very hard to pay attention. Now he lectures to me alone and ignores the rest of the class!"

Students do not realize the power they have to influence their classroom experiences. Through the judicious use of attention and listening skills, students can have more involvement in the direction of their learning than most would consider possible. This experiment demonstrates the joint responsibility of teacher and student for what goes on inside the classroom.

Middle-class students often develop the skills of being a successful student naturally. Other students, particularly those from disadvantaged backgrounds, have not learned the behavioral dimensions of "studenting." Microtraining procedures offer an avenue to teach students some aspects of successful academic work.

MICROTRAINING TECHNIQUES WITH MENTAL PATIENTS

One view of the hospitalized mental patient is that he is an individual with a behavioral deficit rather than an "ill" or "sick" person. In such a view, the patient is seen as lacking behavioral skills and alternatives. The treatment of choice then becomes supplying the individual with a variety of alternative behaviors which he may adapt to better his situation. The literature on behavior modification contains many examples of how specific behaviors can be taught or produced in the hospitalized mental patient.

Donk (1969) adapted the microtraining framework to instruct hospitalized mental patients in the skill of attending behavior. He used the basic microcounseling training format to teach this skill and found that patients could readily learn listening skills. Further, he rated ward behavior and found that patients who had learned attending behavior demonstrated improved ward adjustment as compared to nontreatment controls.

Freiband and Rudman (1970) have explored the uses of media therapy (Higgins, Ivey, and Uhlemann, 1970) with hospitalized patients and clinically demonstrated that it is possible to teach patients a variety of behavioral skills. In an impressive demonstration, a chronic schizophrenic, who had been in the hospital a full year without improvement, was taught attending behavior, nonverbal behavioral control, and self-expression skills. In early sessions, this patient responded to questions inappropriately. "How do you feel toward authority?", for example, was answered with, "I want to get a driver's license." In addition, a good deal of nervous twitching and movement was apparent. When the patient viewed the first videotape, he was able to comment that he "didn't listen very well" and "jiggled too much." Microtraining sessions were supplemented by specific reinforcements arranged according to a time sequence. The patient was asked a question, and if he responded inappropriately or within the first five seconds he lost five cents. If he waited five seconds and responded appropriately he received five cents. Over ten seconds, the patient again had to pay the therapists.

At first, the patient lost money, but within one week he was winning most of the time. At this point, the financial incentives were eliminated and replaced by the more usual social incentives of microtraining. Three weeks after beginning microtraining, this patient was seeking a job in the community (microtraining was also used to help him prepare for the first job interviews), and he was subsequently released.

Currently, Freiband and Ivey are considering amplifications of the media therapy and microcounseling frameworks for the behavioral instruction of mental patients. Important in this work is the involvement of patients in selecting behaviors that they would like to change. Microtraining techniques have also been used to facilitate patient communication with their families and as a supplement to group therapy procedures.

MICROTRAINING WITH PARAPROFESSIONALS

Haase and DiMattia (1970) utilized the microcounseling paradigm to train counseling paraprofessionals in the skills of attending behavior, expression of feeling, and reflection of feeling. Many counselor trainees have trouble recognizing and reflecting feelings to their clients. Haase and DiMattia found that teaching paraprofessionals to recognize and express personal feelings was helpful in their later performance in recognizing others' emotions.

Another important innovation of this study was the use of small groups for microtraining. Trainees were paired and then videotaped; they interviewed one another while the remainder of the group watched. Instead of individual instruction and feedback, group supervision was used. While trainees did not achieve full competence in their first sessions, research data revealed markedly improved performance in the skills in question.

A follow-up study one year later (Haase, DiMattia, and Guttman, 1970) examined the degree to which the specific skills were maintained. It was found that the paraprofessionals retained improved nonverbal communication and ability to express feelings. However, verbal following and reflection-of-feeling statements decreased, although remaining above original performance levels. The authors concluded that the environment in which the paraprofessionals were working did not reinforce counseling-type behavior, and the behavior learned during original training was eventually partially extinguished. They suggest the need for adequate follow-up, supervision, and practical experience if learned behaviors are to be fully maintained.

Cowles (1970) explored the microtraining framework with mental health paraprofessionals in a junior college. He did not preselect skills, but instead had each trainee briefly interview a volunteer client. Trainees were asked to select the skills on which they would like to improve. Individual behavioral training programs were devised where necessary. Clinical observation revealed that this was an especially successful and popular feature of the training program.

PREPARATION FOR JOB INTERVIEWS

Keil (1968) developed a detailed plan for training groups of mental patients in job interviewing skills in two four-hour periods. The first period focused on application forms, dress and appearance, appropriate mannerisms, and an "asset search."

Patients learned how to explain hospitalization and their past history. In each area, the patient role-played possible ways of handling situations with employers. Videotaped models of appropriate behavior were presented, against which the patient could compare himself.

The second two-hour session focused specifically on the job interview. Patients role-played a minimum of two job interviews. Positive and negative behaviors were identified and positive reinforcement for appropriate behavior was given by the trainer.

While formal research data on this program is not available, some patients previously judged "hard core and unemployable" by the placement office of the hospital found jobs after training.

DiMattia (1970) has used an individual approach to teach college students skills of presenting themselves successfully in an employment interview. A wide variety of interview situations could use adaptations of the microtraining framework to assist individuals to meet others more effectively.

ADAPTATIONS OF MICROCOUNSELING IN
SELF-UNDERSTANDING WORKSHOPS

Malamud (1971) has developed self-confrontation group techniques which he uses in Self-Understanding Workshops where members create from amongst themselves "second chance families." These "families" attempt to provide members with a second chance at growth opportunities which may not have been present in their actual childhood families. Utilizing the behavioral concepts of microcounseling, he developed interesting affective exercises to facilitate communication which are quoted below:*

> I am developing a number of training exercises which aim at stimulating members to recognize their habitual interactional patterns and/or practice new and potentially more useful responses to each other. Some of the examples below have been inspired by Ivey's ingenious microteaching of effective relationship behaviors, an

---

* Reprinted from Blank, L., and Gottesegen, G., and Gottesegen, M. (Eds.): *Encounter: Confrontations in Self and Interpersonal Awareness.* Copyright by The Macmillan Company. Used by permission of The Macmillan Company.

approach in which human relations skills to be taught are reduced to manageable units that are practiced one at a time.

Get it Off Your Chest. I divide the group into trios, and a circle of these trios is formed. One member in each trio is designated A, the second, B, and the third, C. I tell the A's to share with their B's something disturbing that they are experiencing in relation to the Workshop, for example, an upsetting occurrence, some worry about what might happen in the Workshop, or a negative reaction to a classmate or the leader. All B students are instructed to respond to the A's in ways which make A feel that he is really being listened to and that an effort is being made to understand how he feels. All C students are told to observe the interactions between A's and B's with particular attention to evaluating the ways in which B's appear to fulfill their assignment. Student A and student B interact for five minutes, and then each trio takes five minutes to share its observations and reactions. Then all A's move in a clockwise direction, and all C's in a counterclockwise direction, to the next trio. In this fashion every member becomes part of a new trio. B's now share their disturbances while C's and A's observe. Then in a third shifting of trios the A's express their disturbances. This exercise is useful in giving members practice in expressing disturbed feelings, and in providing training in some of the listening skills they will require in their family interactions.

Sharing Feelings. I tell the group, "I have to present a paper at a professional meeting this Saturday, and I feel scared to death," I ask each member to respond to me with a single sentence. I reply to each sentence with either an 'Ugh' or a "Thank you." For example, if somebody says to me, "You shouldn't be nervous. After all, you're a psychologist!" I answer, "Ugh! I don't want to talk to you anymore." But if, on the other hand, a student in the group says to me, "Gee, I have felt that way too," I say, "Thank you. I'd like to tell you more." So I go around in this way. It is a simple thing, but they get the point: Some ways of responding may turn people off, and other ways may encourage further self-disclosure. After I have modeled this exercise, I ask for a volunteer to take my place with a self-disclosure of his own.

In a variation of this exercise, I divide the group into two subgroups, A and B. I place myself in group A. I express a feeling, for example, "I don't know why, but I just don't like to be touched." I tell members in group A, "Each of you pretend that this is your feeling, and that you have just expressed it. Now each member in group B will respond in turn to this feeling of yours with a single sentence. See whether this sentence makes you feel closer to or more distant from the responding person. If closer, raise your hand.

The number of raised hands constitutes the 'score' for each responder." For example, following are two B members' quite different responses to the above feeling with their scores in parentheses: "OK, I won't touch you." (5) "You have a right not to like being touched, but perhaps talking about it might help." (12) After each member in group A has presented a feeling for response from group B, the two groups exchange roles, and people in the B group offer feelings to be responded to by the A group (Malamud, 1971).

Malamud's imaginative work is especially relevant, as it underlines the fact that *the microtraining framework is only one route toward accomplishing a specific goal.* If we wish to teach another person attending behavior or self-expressive behaviors, the microcounseling framework is just one viable training alternative. Single behavioral skills can be taught in many ways. If a person has the desire, he can learn attending behavior or psychological interpretation skills simply by reading about them or hearing someone else talk about them.

However, most individuals learn quickly and efficiently in a stimulating situation. Many can learn behavior skills via microtraining, but there are other routes to learning these skills. Exercises such as Malamud's are especially appropriate and effective means.

MICROTRAINING WITH COMMUNITY YOUTH PROGRAMS

Zeevi (1970a, b) has instituted microtraining as a regular part of the Jewish Community Center of Springfield, Massachusetts. He has used attending behavior concepts in three different areas, (a) leadership training programs for teenagers, (b) training leaders for the Center's day-camp program, and (c) to train volunteers for the "hot line," a telephone counseling and referral service for teens operated by Springfield College.

Zeevi has made an effort to blend dyadic experience in microtraining with group process. Dyadic instruction follows group training procedures similar to those employed by Haase with paraprofessionals. Each trainee alternately acts as a listener and an expressor and obtains feedback from the group and the supervisor. Zeevi has found that the physical dimensions of attending behavior have been well received by teenagers and has also found that listening skills learned in this setting have generalized to home situations.

He also has used informal group exercises in self-expressive and attending behavior. An example is a case of one teenager who spoke to the group for five minutes. Following his presentation, he received feedback on his verbal and nonverbal behavior as he was talking to the group. He then gave the group feedback on how he perceived them as listeners. In a later session, both he and the group changed certain behaviors—he looked at them as he talked (prior to that he looked above them), he moved physically more and used his hands less. Members of the group faced him, sat towards him and used more facial expressions as he talked. He also lowered his voice. After the second attempt, one of the girls who goes to school with him said: "First it was a game. I participated with the others. Then as you talked and looked at me and lowered your voice I forgot that this is an exercise. I really liked it . . . you were cool." Another boy from the same class added: "I wish you'd do it in class too." The boy was rather embarrassed and at the same time seemed also very pleased with himself. It seems that he plays the role of the joker in class and here he was told how others can like him without him always playing a stereotyped role.

TRAINING FOR COUNSELING CLIENTS

Haase, Forsyth, Julius, and Lee (1969) adapted the microtraining paradigm to teach clients accurate expression of feelings prior to initiation of counseling. Prospective cilents were assigned to the following three groups: microtraining, regular intake interview, and no intake interview, and it was found that the trained group expressed more emotion in the first session of actual counseling.

Truax (1965, 1966) found that listening to an audio recording of a counseling session in which a client illustrated how to explore feelings moderately increased gains from counseling. Haase *et al.* suggest that the reinforcement of specific behaviors encouraged in microtraining may further facilitate client growth. In situations where clients have a deficit in their ability to express themselves, microcounseling training can be especially suitable. The authors suggest that it might be appropriate to develop a program of generalized behaviors which are facilitative to client growth in most types of therapy and counseling; in addition, they speculate on the possibility of individualized training programs for clients who may encounter therapists with varying orientations.

Studying the application of models to facilitate encounter groups, Whalen (1969) found that viewing videotapes of small groups who made a large number of open interpersonal statements led to increased interpersonal openness at a later time. While Whalen's study focused on the use of models to facilitate performance, the possibility of adapting her work to facilitate encounter groups through microtraining should be considered. Stoller (1965) has demonstrated that videotaping encounter sessions is useful in facilitating group movement.

Supplementing this suggestion is the possibility of referring individuals who have difficulties relating to the group process to microtraining and then returning them to the regular group. For example, a group often demonstrates at a profound level that an individual cannot listen to others' feelings. However, they usually do not tell him what behaviors he should engage in to change himself. Referral for microtraining in specific skills may be useful because it can provide skills or alternatives which the individual can use to facilitate self-change. Simultaneously, group pressure may motivate an individual to learn a new behavior where before he would not have been interested.

While client pretraining may be useful, a more economical use of resources is to have videotape microtraining programs available to the counselor who might refer his client for training in specific behavioral skills needed by the client. For example, it is possible to use training in attending behavior to help clients who have difficulty in talking to others. Training in reflection and expression of feeling has proven helpful to those in marital counseling.

MICROTRAINING AND CO-COUNSELING SUPERVISION

Thielen (1970) has developed an interesting program to teach counselors-in-training to increase their use of accurate empathic responses in a counseling interview. His method is a three-hour session in which the counseling supervisor, the trainee, and counselee work together for mutual facilitation.

The thirty-minute presession includes only the supervisor and trainee. The trainee reads a written manual on accurate empathy, views a tape with three levels of empathy demonstrated, and role-plays empathy. The supervisor and his trainee then plan for the upcoming session and discuss how they can use the tri-relationship for "maximum help for all concerned." Next, the trainee and supervisor hold a thirty minute co-counseling session with the client. During this session, both operate as counselors and seek to develop an understanding of the client. The supervisor and the trainee hold a thirty-minute postsession in which the trainee rates the supervisor's and his own behavior against the description in the written manual. Role playing of specific behaviors and appropriate feedback are part of this session. If necessary, the models of empathy are again shown.

A second thirty-minute co-counseling session is then held with the client. Near the end of this session, the client is encouraged to give feedback to the trainee. A final postsession of forty-five minutes reviews the entire procedure and stresses the skills taught within the session.

This procedure was found to facilitate trainee ability to respond in standardized counseling situations and also increased the trainee's self-concept.

Thielen's use of microtraining techniques in conjunction with co-counseling, the complex counseling skill of empathy, and the actual counseling of a client illustrates an interesting modification of the basic microtraining framework. The juxtaposition of different media and approaches seems a particularly promising avenue for counselor training, especially when complex skills of therapy are under consideration.

A COMPREHENSIVE APPROACH TO A SINGLE INTERVIEW

Greenall (1969) has developed a series of short videotape excerpts which represent positive and negative behavioral models of various phases of the interview. Section one of his videotape focuses on beginning the interview and presents models of positive and negative seating relationships, listening to client's viewpoints, and noting the client's feeling. Each specific point is identified by commentary.

Section two of the tape focuses on observing the client's nonverbal communications while section three focuses on responding to the client. In these sections, listening and questioning skills are stressed. The final section of the tape illustrates methods of summarizing the interview, giving advice, and terminating the session. Greenall used this tape and adaptations of the microcounseling paradigm to train manpower counselors for the Canadian Department of Manpower and Immigration.

Another important variation in microtraining procedures is demonstrated here. Rather than focusing on single skills and letting the trainee place them into a larger framework at a later point, Greenall provides a structure wherein the trainee may actually see the relevance and place of specific skills in the actual interview setting. A particular danger of the single tape, however, is that the trainee can be overwhelmed by too much data or information on what he should do. Our experience has been that even the most talented trainee can absorb only so much at one time. This was also Greenall's experience. In a revised edition of his program, Greenall treated each section of the tape as a complete program in itself, and more time was spent focusing on the specific skills he wanted to convey to the trainee. Each section builds on the previous section.

Used in this way, Greenall's method could be a particularly promising one. It may be desirable to combine the broad conceptual framework he suggests with the single-skills approach. As trainees learn the skills of introduction to the interview, they can continue sequentially to later phases.

Similarly, it should be possible to utilize the microtraining framework to develop programs in conjunction with specific therapeutic orientations. Although perhaps unlikely to see the light of day, it would be possible to develop a comprehensive set of models and materials on the processes of long-term psychoanalysis. Such a series could focus on basic analytic constructs and present positive and negative models on how the therapist handles situations. A variety of counseling orientations from behavior modification through existentialism could be taught, utilizing microtraining procedures. Regardless of the orientation selected, a systematic selection of skills seems appropriate. The skills suggested in this book were selected as representing generalized counseling and interviewing skills that can be useful in more than one therapeutic situation. It is anticipated that for maximum benefit, they may be placed as part of a larger, more comprehensive theoretical orientation.

MICROCOUNSELING IN A COLLEGE UNDERGRADUATE COURSE

Schwebel (1970) has utilized four microcounseling skills in his undergraduate course of approximately eighty students, "Introduction to Clinical Psychology." The first assignment given to the class is to outline "what a clinical psychologist would have to know about you in order to begin to understand you." Schwebel states that this is then discussed among the students in small groups and used by them as a basis on which to develop interviewing topics useful in understanding others. Before their first interview with a fellow student, microcounseling manuals are introduced. Interviewing and the interviewer then become the focus of discussion for the following two weeks.

Some student comments on the utility and value of microcounseling in this course follow:

> I read through the microcounseling manuals before I did my interview and they helped to relax me. I was really a nervous wreck and I had no idea how or where to start. They helped me formulate some questions and they were a check on the kinds of questions I had thought about asking. I tried to follow the ideas for physically adjusting to the counseling situation. I found that by having this to concentrate on in the beginning that the interview went more

smoothly and I could soon be more natural.

The microcounseling hints given for good interviewing or easy-going conversation with a client are very basic ideas. There is nothing astounding about them; in fact they are the sort of things I would do anyway . . . To me, these hints were just a matter of course that do not even need to be told.

The material is valuable in preparing one for interviewing, especially as a beginner . . . Often, as I am an inexperienced interviewer, the interviewee would question my feelings and opinions, and I was somewhat lost as to how to handle the situation. Thus, I felt it useful to have skills which enabled me to redirect the session back to the interviewee.

I found the microcounseling papers interesting. The reading was easy and they were very informative. However, only so much can be learned from reading and the practical experience of interviews under the guidance of the professor was most valuable.

If the interviewer tries to use micro skills in only two interviews, he can't establish these skills as automatic habits. However, if one tries to use them from time to time in various situations, they would be more valuable. Fortunately, the micro skills are clear, so it is difficult to abuse them too much. There are several good ways to abuse these skills, however, by using the skills at the wrong time or using them inappropriately . . . When watching an individual who is a "listener," one can see that many of the micro skills are natural to these individuals. The micro skills are not just something placed on a conversation, but are derived from observations of successful listeners and therapists in conversations.

These student comments illustrate the ability of undergraduate students to conceptualize important issues in microtraining. Perhaps particularly important in their development in the course was the combination of informal small groups plus specific, more behavioral material for them to consider. It seems clear from the above examples that some benefited more from the experience with microtraining than others, yet all had the opportunity to look at counseling and therapy from a new point of view.

Models such as that provided by Schwebel may be important in communicating counseling skills to large numbers of people. His innovative approach is one which deserves further consideration and research.

ALTERNATIVE USES OF MICROTRAINING

The above suggestions, extensive in variation and implications, are only a brief summary of the potential uses of the microtraining framework. Other interesting adaptations of the microcounseling framework include the following examples.

Danish (1970) trained one large group consisting of 250 dormitory counselors in direct, mutual communication. The counselors divided into dyads and talked for five minutes. An adaptation of the programmed text was passed out and an experienced couple demonstrated various types of open communication on the stage. The dyads then discussed among themselves how their session compared with the model and the text. A second and third five-minute session were then conducted. During the session, a roving group of previously trained counselors met with groups around the room.

Bloom (1970) did not have videotape equipment available for training of social workers in interviewing skills. As such, he rewrote two training manuals (attending behavior and reflection of feeling) and used role playing and discussion methods in groups of three, supported by faculty members of the graduate school of social work, University of Indiana. In these groups, the third person served as the feedback mechanism. Each step in learning proved to be a group experience, and "students became quite aware of themselves and quite adept as critics of others." Too often, interviewing is a lonely process in which the individual does not reveal to others how his sessions progress. Bloom's training may have special benefit for a new generation of interviewers who are more willing to share their problems and methods with one another.

Aldrige (1970) is currently completing research on teaching junior high school students the skills of attending behavior via a microtraining format. Observation of tapes and early data reveals that this younger population can be taught the skills of microtraining as easily as older, more experienced adults. Many junior high school students are shy and cannot talk to members of the opposite sex easily. Training in attending behavior and skills of self-expression appears to be useful to these youngsters. Aldrige has also employed the teaching of specific communication skills as a basic part of family therapy programs with the disadvantaged. He has taught mothers of "problem children" basic attending skills, or put more simply, how they can listen to their children. Aldrige points out that ghetto parents often do not have sufficient behavioral skills to communicate with their children and the imparting of attending behavior has on occasion provided the first family communication in years.

Microtraining has also been adapted with some success for executive training programs in industry. It has been proposed as a system of sales training in an insurance company. Similarly, it would appear to be a useful method to teach distributive education students (sales trainees in high school who are released part of the day) basic business skills.

Direct, mutual communication has been found to be useful as a skill to facilitate marital communication, and it would seem that this, plus other microtraining skills, might be useful as a supplement to marriage counseling or as an addendum to marriage and the family courses in college and high school.

In an experimental program, the Dade County school system in Miami, Florida (Collins, 1970), taught attending skills to a group of high school students who serve as teacher aides. These students are assisting English teachers and are teaching attending behavior to fellow students as part of their duties.

The utility of the microtraining model in clinical speech pathology is currently being explored by Irwin (1970). Special attention is being paid to the skills required in supervising beginning speech therapists. In this way, the validity of the microtraining model will be tested with an important group of helpers—speech therapists. The study involves a complex design and includes an examination of videotapes of speech therapy sessions themselves. Results from this study will be valuable not only to those who work in speech but also to those interested in further examination of the microtraining process.

LaFrance (1970) has applied the microcounseling model to train counselors in a faculty-student drug education and counseling center. He has found that the specific skills of microtraining are taught most effectively as an adjunct to group process. When a specific issue in drug education or treatment comes up and the need for a specific skill is apparent, LaFrance employs on-the-spot microtraining with videotape equipment. He has found that the immediate use of the framework has been effective in imparting counseling skills. He states that more traditional forms of microtraining have proven less successful and that these students feel a greater sense of immediacy and involvement in training through this more spontaneous method.

There appear to be a multitude of possible uses and adaptations of all or part of the microtraining paradigm. Such changes, however, must be based in their relevance and appropriateness for the group involved. It would be easy to suggest that virtually any area of human endeavor can be broken down into identifiable skills and that the skills can be taught with measurable results. However, while microtraining and microcounseling are useful methods of instruction, they are not the only methods nor are they necessarily an effective way of instruction for all people in all settings. Rather, it is more reasonable to see the microtraining framework as another vehicle to impart information and realize that like all other teaching vehicles, the quality of the teacher or supervisor is ultimately the most important dimension. The injunction that the supervisor himself must model the skills he is teaching (be congruent) must again be emphasized.

Chapter Seven

RESEARCH IMPLICATIONS OF MICROTRAINING

THE CHIEF BARRIER to meaningful research in interviewing, counseling, and psychotherapy is the complex nature of the interaction. It is difficult to systematize the many variables occurring between two individuals over one session, to say nothing of a series of interviews in long-term psychotherapy. Process and outcome research in interviewing has been handicapped by an inability to spell out variables in detail and to relate antecedent and consequent events. Recent contributions by the behavior therapists (c.f. Gendlin and Rychlak, 1970; Phillips and Kanfer, 1969) have done much to clarify issues, but many problems of research and evaluation remain.

The microtraining paradigm provides a controlled, systematic, laboratory setting in which the dyadic interview process can be studied under naturalistic conditions. The tenor of the actual counseling session remains, but the specificity made possible by the nature of microtraining provides an opportunity for more careful delineation of what occurs in interviewing sessions. In addition, behaviors manifested in microtraining may be identified and quantified and then related to the generalization of these behaviors beyond the microtraining sessions.

This chapter summarizes some of the research uses for microtraining. Three main areas are identified for consideration. These are (a) the utility of the framework for identifying new behavioral skills for the interviewer or his client, (b) methods of evaluating the comparative effectiveness of microtraining and other training systems, and (c) the potential of microtraining as a controlled situation for research on dyadic interaction.

IDENTIFYING BEHAVIORAL SKILLS

The most obvious research use of microtraining is in identifying and labeling discrete behavioral skills of interviewing. Twelve specific skills have been suggested and experimented with thus far, and as suggested earlier, they are only a beginning to the many possibilities for research. There is a need for identification of additional skills, especially as they relate to specific problems of the interview and to differing theoretical persuasions.

Originally, developing new interview skills proved to be a difficult and time-consuming process. However, out of these efforts has developed a straightforward and workable method which provides a more efficient use of time. Production of the video modeling tape is most crucial in the development of a new skill of interviewing. Once a satisfactory modeling tape is produced, written manuals and conceptual frameworks follow rather easily. This procedure, a "do it first and then think about it" approach, follows these steps:

1. A general idea of the skill is developed and agreed to by the research staff. Extensive discussions or criticisms of the skill are not conducted until the skill is seen on videotape.
2. A negative model is videotaped, and a deliberate effort is made to demonstrate the absence of the skill in question. In developing reflection of feeling, for example, an effort was made to ignore all feelings expressed by the client.
3. The model is reviewed, the specific negative behaviors are labeled, and behaviors for a positive model of the skill are identified.
4. A positive modeling tape is produced. This, combined with the negative tape, provides a framework for final production of the skill, the written manual, and eventual research specifications.

Identification is the first step in determining the validity of a skill. The next step involves training others in the same skill. Unless the skill can be demonstrated as transferable to new trainees as a discrete unit, it probably does not actually exist.

To date, most microcounseling research has focused on the development and transferability of skills.

In teaching others the new skill, the traditional microcounseling model has been utilized. Trend analysis design with repeated measures of a single treatment group, control or comparison designs, and multiple comparison groups have all been utilized to determine the reality of a skill. The use of multiple comparison groups has proven most fruitful. Carkhuff (1969b) has outlined one very useful design. Figure 1 presents an adaptation of his paradigm.*

Carkhuff notes the following:

> The pre-treatment and post-treatment test administrations allow us to asesss the effects of our treatment over time. We need to have an estimate of the helpee's initial level of functioning on the relevant indexes in order to determine the degree of change on these indexes . . . different treatment and control groups allow us to distinguish the effects of treatment from the effects of many other ongoing experiences. Therefore, the treatment of preference will be incorporated in one group called the treatment proper or experimental group. A second group, termed the control group, will receive no treatment . . . A third group, and this is perhaps the most important, will receive the same special attention as the treatment group for the same amount and duration of time. If possible, this group will receive all of the aspects of the treatment proper except for those characteristics that are most critical to the treatment . . . there must be some assurance that the individuals in the different groups are equivalent on the relevant dimensions. This may be accomplished by random assignment or matching. It is also crucial that the helpers or trainers be matched in their level of functioning on relevant dimensions.

This long quote has been inserted because it summarizes most of the issues we have discovered in microcounseling research. The trend-analysis design employed in some microtraining research involves pretesting and posttesting and, in some cases, follow-up testing as well. While subjects have

---

* Adapted and reprinted from *Helping and Human Relations: A Primer for Lay and Professional Helpers*, Vol. II, by Robert R. Carkhuff. Copyright 1969 by Holt, Rinehart, and Winston, Inc. Used by permission of Holt, Rinehart, and Winston, Inc.

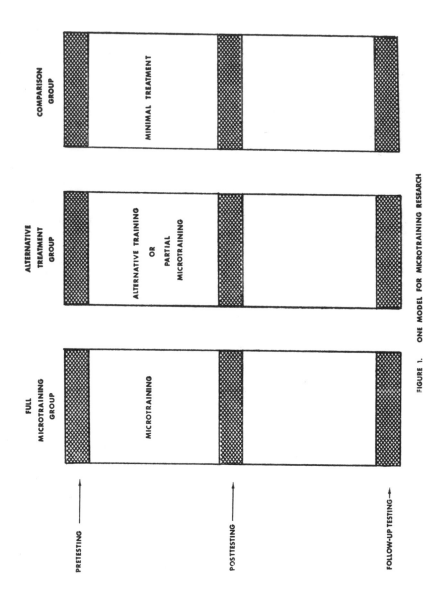

FIGURE 1.   ONE MODEL FOR MICROTRAINING RESEARCH

demonstrated improvement and retained skills over periods of time, the lack of comparison groups handicaps this method. Higgins, Ivey, and Uhlemann (1970) and Kelley (1970) have employed the design suggested by Carkhuff and found that it provides maximum information for effort involved.

Microtraining research has only recently reached the stage whereby adequate follow-up testing has been possible. Studies by Haase, DiMattia, and Guttman (1970), Miller, Morrill, Ivey, Normington, and Uhlemann (1969) and Moreland, Phillips, Ivey, and Lockhart (1970) revealed that trainees have retained the skills learned over time. Hutchcraft (1970), however, found fairly rapid extinction of skills learned. Considerable additional work is called for in examining the retention and generalization of microtraining skills. Bandura (1969) has indicated that retention of learned behavior is greatly enhanced by practice in the life environment. Probably, retention of microtraining skills depends on the clarity with which the skill is first learned and on subsequent opportunities to gain further experience with that skill.

Developing functionally meaningful indices to test the development of identified behavioral skills has not been as difficult as one might suppose. The first study on attending behavior (Ivey *et al.*, 1968) utilized a five-point rating scale (reliability .84) of five specific behavioral dimensions. Similar five-point scales have been used with consistently satisfactory reliability. The five-point rating scales were not originally designed after Carkhuff's (1969b) five-point interpersonal process scales, but recent examination reveals important correspondence between the two approaches. The specific behaviors of microtraining are closely related to Carkhuff's concept of facilitative conditions. In effect, microtraining skills, by their very nature, assist and facilitate the growth of others.

While rating scales of interview process have proven consistently effective, other evaluation approaches have been used. In the original attending behavior study, a typescript was completed on all sessions and rated for verbal attending behavior by two trained raters. If a counselor comment followed the verbal comments of the client, it was scored plus. If it did not follow, it was scored minus. Of 1,904 ratings, the two raters disagreed on only 114. In this method, each counselor is scored for the percentage of verbal attending behavior in each session.

Other measures used in microcounseling studies include adaptions of the affectivity-sensitivity scale (Kagan and Krathwohl, 1967), counselor self-concept ratings, variations of semantic differential scales, talk-time ratios, mean duration of utterance of counselors, and the Therapist Error Check List (Matarazzo, Phillips, Wiens, and Saslow, 1965). Recently, direct behavioral counts have been employed by Aldrige (1970), and he reports reliabilities of .90 or better on such dimensions as number of breaks in eye contact and number of hand movements. Important in Aldrige's success was a carefully planned eight-hour training series for his raters.

In a more complex but promising approach, Crowley and Ivey (1970) made typescripts of the Higgins, Ivey, Uhlemann (1970) study of the skill of direct, mutual communication. Statements were randomly selected from the first and third five-minute sessions and presented on audiotape to 98 college students. The raters scored each selected comment on a five-point "Interpersonal Process Scale," an adaptation of the Carkhuff (1969b) facilitative conditions scales. The ratings were then factor analyzed to determine what types of comments were most facilitative to interpersonal interaction. This study dramatically reaffirmed the original study's conclusion of the effectiveness of this training method. The raters scored the session following training markedly higher in facilitative conditions.

Factor analytic study revealed nearly twenty factors in both pretraining and posttraining sessions, each accounting for about eighty per cent of the variance. The major difference in verbal statements after training in direct, mutual communication proved to focus on increased reference to the individuals engaged in the process of communication (e.g. statements containing the pronouns "I" and "you") as opposed to references to things or abstract topics. There was also a marked increase in the "degree of emotional expressiveness." Factors containing words connoting love, fear, and anger were virtually nonexistent in the pretraining session; such words were evident in thirteen of seventeen factors from the final session.

Additional specific examples of comments considered by the raters have been identified. As a next step, it is proposed that those factors now labeled as more effective be incorporated into training programs in direct, mutual communication. For example, instructions could include suggestions such as "Use your partner's name in every sentence," or "Include as many emotionally loaded words as you can in your interaction." It might be anticipated that such instructions, being even more specific than the present program in direct, mutual communication, might lead to better learning and retention of the skills involved in this study.

The study outlined above was an adaptation of the work of Zimmer and Park (1967). They used Strupp's (1960) simple warm-cold five-point scale and had 75 respondents classify 100 counselor statements contained in each of two interviews. The correlation matrix for each set of 100 statements was factor analyzed, followed by varimax rotation. Statements loading highly on ten and seven factors respectively were easily interpretable and all but one of the second session's factors correspond to those of the first. Interestingly, the identified factors correspond closely to some of the microtraining skills developed as extensions of the attending behavior construct and described in Chapter Four. The factors identified by Zimmer and Park were restating and understanding, minimal activity-present cognitive, minimal activity-future affective, unstructured invitation, reflection of school conflict, supportive communications, clarification, probing, cognitive interpretation, and affective interpretation. Zimmer and Anderson (1968), using positive regard and empathy scales, again identified similar components.

The work of Zimmer and his associates, when coupled with the microtraining study of Crowley and Ivey, suggests the feasibility of this method for discovering new microtraining skills. Once a verbal construct has been identified through factor-analytic techniques, it is possible to develop a teaching methodology and include it in training protocols. It should be possible to apply such methods not only to verbal constructs of superior model therapists of varying theoretical orientations, but also to nonverbal behavioral aspects of the session, such as body movements and eye contact patterns.

New skills can be developed under the microtraining format, using a variety of methods. Most common have been observational methods in which positive or negative interviewers' behavior is defined and codified under a systematic framework. Factor-analytic techniques such as those discussed above provide another source for identifying new skills and for testing the validity of already existing skills. Techniques as varying as systematic desensitization, encounter groups, and psychoanalytic transference and countertransference issues could be considered relevant for examination within the microtraining format. Not only would such examination help identify the behavioral components of these now somewhat mystical approaches, but it would make direct instruction possible in the specific techniques of some very powerful approaches to human behavior change.

THE EFFECTIVENESS OF MICROTRAINING

A study by Moreland, Phillips, Ivey and Lockhart (1970) provides a basic model for studying the effectiveness of microtraining. Ten beginning clinical psychology graduate students were videotaped while interviewing a patient for thirty minutes. During the ensuing semester, they received intensive microtraining in six skills (attending behavior, minimal encourages, open invitation, reflection of feeling, summarization, and paraphrasing). At the end of the semester, the trainees interviewed the same patient for another thirty minutes. Specific interviewing skills and more general interview effectiveness were evaluated.

Counselor responses were codified by two independent raters into separate categories representing the six skills. Open invitation, reflection of feeling and summarization increased both quantitatively and qualitatively. The attending-behavior scale revealed significant improvement. The number of closed-ended questions was reduced, while the number of minimal encourages and paraphrases remained the same. It was also found that the trainees decreased in the number of errors on the Therapist Error

Checklist (Matarazzo, Phillips, Wiens, and Saslow, 1965). There was, however, no decrease in the number and duration of counselor utterances. These data suggest that the trainees were more effective interviewers after microtraining and that the specific behaviors they had learned became integrated into their skill repertoire.

This study, however, may represent more of a methodological model for counseling research than a true test of the effectiveness of microtraining. The lack of a control group limits the degree to which the microtraining processes can be recommended for use with other training programs. As such, Moreland, Phillips, and Ivey are currently extending the methods of this study using psychiatric trainees as subjects.

Haase, DiMattia, and Guttman (1970) conducted a one year follow-up study of paraprofessional trainees who had been trained in attending behavior, expression of feeling, and reflection of feeling (Haase and DiMattia, 1970). They found nonverbal aspects of attending behavior and the verbal construct of expression of feeling still high. However, verbal following and reflection-of-feeling ratings, while still higher than prior to training, had regressed.

The authors concluded that the paraprofessionals had not received on-the-job reinforcement for these listening behaviors. They suggest the need to examine the environmental situation and to provide mechanisms through which newly learned behavior may be practiced and rewarded. These results may be compared to the Moreland, Phillips, Ivey, and Lockhart (1970) study in which more behaviors related to counseling were taught over a longer period of time with more opportunity for practice and subsequent reinforcement. In the later study, the evidence is that the learned behaviors were maintained and integrated into the interview in a meaningful fashion.

Kelley (1970) trained beginning counselors in specific skills of the interview, as suggested by Matarazzo and Wiens (1967). Using a modified microcounseling format, he found that the two trained groups when compared to a control group had done the following: (a) significantly reduced the number of and length of utterances, (b) lowered their percentage of talk time, and (c) reduced the number of interruptions. One of the trained groups had the advantage of supervision, while the other went through a carefully designed self-supervision model. Generally, differences between these two models did not appear. However, the supervised group manifested a significantly longer response-time latency and talked less than the self-supervision group.

Hutchcraft (1970), teaching similar skills, found that the microcounseling model was a force for change on four variables—frequency of counselor interruptions, frequency of counselor zero response latency, total number of counselor responses, and total duration of counselor talk time. Hutchcraft's study included an examination of varying modeling procedures and retention of the learned skills. He found that individuals trained with the most complete modeling procedure learned the skills most effectively but that the skills were not maintained over a twenty-four hour delay period. Hutchcraft concluded that there is need for applied practice in learned skills following training.

The studies by Kelley and Hutchcraft are especially valuable as they bring the microcounseling approach together with the well-defined behavioral variables of Matarazzo and his colleagues. They have demonstrated that the microcounseling paradigm has utility in frameworks beyond those suggested specifically in this book. This work also suggests some important variables for examining the long-term effectiveness of micro-counseling.

Much of counseling research has relied on generalized ratings of the effectiveness of the interview. Only recently have be-havioral counts of counselor actions been introduced. The model of the studies cited above may prove a useful one for examining the interviewing process since they combine broad ratings of interview effectiveness with observable behavioral dimensions.

We have not yet examined the question of whether micro-training is a more effective method of counseling training than others. Regardless of the comparative effectiveness of different training modalities, some individuals will learn interviewing more effectively under one system and others under another system. One route to achieve the objectives of the competent inter-viewer, counselor, or therapist may be microtraining. Other important potential routes are interpersonal process recall (Kagan and Krathwohl, 1967), affect simulation (Kagan and Schauble, 1909), relationship emphasis between supervisor and trainee (Kell and Mueller, 1966; Wideman, 1970), direct instruction in behavioral techniques, simulation techniques, computer-assisted counseling (Cooley, 1968; Jones, 1968), personal psychoanalysis, encounter groups, and a host of other alternatives.

Emphasis on the effectiveness of microtraining has thus far focused on behavioral change in the trainee interviewer. *The real test of the effectiveness of an interviewing approach is the impact it has on clients.* Microcounseling research studies have consistently found that trainees are rated more favorably after training on evaluation scales administered pretraining and posttraining. The Counselor Effectiveness Scale (Ivey, Miller, Morrill, Normington, and Haase, 1967), despite its reactivity, has proven to be a sensitive indicator of counselee perceptions of counselors-in-training. This has been further supported by clinical impressions that microtraining clients have enjoyed the experience and even benefited from the short-term counseling provided, particularly in the media therapy study (Higgins, Ivey, Uhlemann, 1970).

Normington (1969) took videotapes of four experienced counselors who had helped develop modeling tapes of reflection of feeling and presented them to two expert counselors and 68 high school students. The experts and students rated each counselor on the Counselor Effectiveness Scale (see Appendix A). It was found that experts and students agreed in their ratings and ranked all four counselors in the same order. Normington noted that the semantic differential items defining the more skilled counselor included high ratings on such words as close, meaningful, helpful, secure, strong, active, industrious, and efficient. The counselor who received lowest ranking received low ratings on words such as deep, close, skillful, competent, meaningful, and helpful.

Normington's work illustrates another possible use of microtraining in research issues. It would be possible to identify counselors rated most effectively by students and experts and then examine the verbal and nonverbal behaviors of each.

Interestingly, there is also preliminary evidence in Normington's work that students and experts both preferred a more active and impactful counselor as opposed to counselors who scored highly on such words as nice, pleasant, and friendly. Further study of this nature should help identify the nature of the impactful counselor, interviewer, or therapist.

The study by Kelley (1970) discussed earlier has important data on client participation in the interview. To repeat, it was found that clients who talked with trained interviewers participated more actively and talked more in the interview. Their mean duration of utterance increased while number and length of counselor utterances decreased. The original attending behavior study (Ivey *et al.*, 1968) found that microcounseling trainees talked 47 percent of the time in the first interview and 33 percent in the second whereas figures for the control group were 42 percent and 37 percent.

The methods employed by Haase, Forsyth, Julius and Lee (1969) in training counseling clients in expression of feeling has potential importance for suggesting additional means of studying the effects of microtraining skills on individuals. They found it possible to codify and rate client participation and behavior in microtraining sessions much as counselor behaviors have been studied in other microtraining sessions. This would seem to suggest that the entire microtraining methodology of noting and codifying specific skills could be applied to the study of clients in the counseling process. It should be possible to systematically study and observe behaviors of clients as their trainee counselors move through alternative microtraining skills.

Such studies might eventually provide answers to questions such as what type of counseling skill is most appropriate with what type of individual and with what type of problem. The systems model for studying counselor education as proposed by Krumboltz and Thoresen (1968) could be applied to the study of clients in the interviewing process. The major issue of the interactive factors of client characteristics and problems, specific client verbal and nonverbal behaviors, and environmental interventions on the part of the interviewer could be studied in detail.

Viewed from a completely different vantage point, clinical

evidence of behavior change should not be discounted as a way to measure the effectiveness of a treatment program. The work of Freiband and Rudman (1970) with hospitalized patients should be cited as an important method of facilitating personal growth. Specific microtraining skills, selected in consultation with the patient, have proven useful in teaching patients listening and self-expression skills and how to solve specific problems such as going through a first job interview. Such clinical uses of microtraining are best described through behavioral charts and clinical case reports. Similarly, interviewing trainees may require individualized approaches which can best meet their own unique needs.

In summary, microcounseling appears to be an effective method of producing behavior change in trainees. While this is most clear in short-term studies of immediate skills, research and clinical evidence is increasing that it also applies to client retention of learned behaviors. Regardless of the effectiveness of these techniques as compared to other methods, the controlled situation of microtraining wherein many variables can be manipulated systematically offers a promising laboratory for study of several important variables in counseling process and outcome.

A CONTROLLED LABORATORY SITUATION FOR RESEARCH

Microtraining is not only a laboratory for the development and identification of skills of interviewing but also serves as a controlled situation wherein many dimensions of the counseling process and dyadic interaction may be studied. With the addition of control or comparison groups, an almost infinite number of hypotheses concerning dyadic or small-group interaction can be tested.

Bandura (1969) has clearly demonstrated the importance of models in the social learning process. Microtraining has demonstrated the value of modeling in learning interviewing and teaching skills. There are many problems in social learning theory which can be explored in systematic detail utilizing the microtraining framework. Among them are such issues as the position and social status of the model, the value of negative versus positive models, and development of programs in which individual differences in response to models may be tested. The last question is especially important because insufficient attention has been paid to individual differences in response to models. For example, discussion of the influence of television in teaching children aggressive and deviant behaviors has not fully considered the fact that some children are more easily molded by models than are others. Microtraining provides a framework wherein individual responses to models may be studied systematically.

Goldberg (1970) examined the comparative effectiveness of audiotape models and instructions in a carefully designed experiment utilizing four groups of thirty students who were to learn the skill of accurate reflection of feeling. The groups were trained with models plus instruction, models only, instructions only, and a placebo experience. Goldberg found that the instructions plus modeling proved most effective in teaching the skill, followed by modeling alone. Interestingly, the instructions-only group was not significantly more successful in producing accurate reflection-of-feeling statements than the control group. It should be noted that Goldberg did not include a supervisor in her study. She concluded, "Since neither videotape nor a supervisor is necessary, it would be possible to teach counseling skills long distance by packaging a series of inexpensive, audiotaped . . . microlessons and sending them to counselors who could learn interviewing skills at home." Wawrykow (1970), when examining video feedback versus audio feedback, found no consistent evidence to favor either approach. He used an adapted microcounseling framework to teach students concepts of facilitative conditions.

Frankel (1970) examined the effects of videotape models and videotape feedback in teaching the microcounseling skill of accurate reflection of feeling. A comparison group received instructions only. Half of the experimental subjects received feedback first and half viewed models first. He found that a combination of videotaped models plus feedback was most effective. Further, he found that showing the model first followed by self-observation produced more positive change.

The study by Hutchcraft (1970), cited earlier, also presented interesting data on the role of models in microtraining. Four groups participated in microtraining. Group one viewed a fifteen-minute videotape of a skilled counselor interviewing a client, followed by a fifteen-minute videotape of a supervisor reinforcing the counselor for his interview performance. Group two viewed only the counselor's tape, group three only the supervisor's tape, and the fourth group viewed none of the models. Each group conducted four interviews and received feedback from their training sessions.

Hutchcraft found that the presentation of the supervisor model provided the most potent force for change. Presentations of the counselor model alone proved less effective. Hutchcraft's study is also important in that it represents another study in which microtraining was conducted without the actual physical presence of a supervisor in the room with the trainee; his evidence suggests that models of the supervision process may be a substitute for actual direct supervision. His findings would support the conclusions of Higgins, Ivey, and Uhlemann (1970) in the media therapy study when they found that presentation of models plus a programmed text could result in significant improvement in behavioral skills.

McDonald and Allen (1967) varied the methods of microtraining treatment in training teachers in a series of controlled studies. They were searching for important variables in microtraining and systematically included or omitted key aspects of the microtraining format such as feedback, modeling, supervision, and instructions. As they note, the clearest finding of their studies was that self-viewing accompanied by supervisor comments was the most powerful aspect of the microtraining treatment. Video modeling tapes proved to be the most effective variables for describing the behavior to be learned. It was found that the presence of a supervisor facilitated learning from the model.

McDonald and Allen reach the general conclusion that the full complement of microtraining methods (feedback, modeling, supervision with cueing and discrimination) was the most effective way to impart skills. If the behavior is relatively simple, they suggest that simple instructions may be sufficient; however, as behavior becomes more complex, the importance of more extensive training seems to appear. Finally, on a more clinical basis, they note that some individuals seem to respond only to certain aspects of the training program, while others seem to prefer the full treatment package.

The studies concerning the comparative effectiveness of models, feedback, supervision and instruction seem together to suggest that maximum treatment results in maximum behavior change. In short, the standard microtraining paradigm appears to be the most effective method of imparting skills. Feedback and self-observation seem the most vital aspect of the program. At the same time, this conclusion must be qualified with the notation that individuals seem to respond differently to microtraining and that adaptations of the model may be required to meet individual wishes and needs. Finally, when behaviors are relatively simple, shortening the basic microtraining framework may be wise. The studies by Goldberg and Wawrykow raise the question of the importance of the videotape medium. While this question is not resolved, it might be suggested that videotape itself may be most important in producing nonverbal changes such as improved eye contact and a more relaxed body posture and gestures, whereas when behaviors are more verbal, audiotape may be equally effective.

Operant conditioning procedures are becoming more prominent as a method of inducing behavior change. Patterson's and Guillian's (1968) important work with reinforcement patterns of families with problem children provides one illustration of the power of this approach. By identifying the mutual reinforcement patterns and distribution of reinforcers in the family, Patterson has been able to assist families in developing more effective relationships. His basic procedure is to identify what is happening in family communication and then to suggest new methods of operant behavior through which individuals might better achieve their objectives. Microtraining offers a controlled situation in which family interaction patterns may be studied and modifications introduced.

A host of other possibilities may be identified for study,

utilizing parts of the microtraining paradigm and adapting operant approaches. Among them are study of the dyadic inter-action to identify patterns of reinforcement in married couples, teaching clients to reinforce counselors for facilitative counsel-ing leads, and manipulations of verbal interaction in the inter-view. Nonverbal cues and body language could be systematically studied in microtraining, and the important issue of individual differences in response to nonverbal cues could be examined.

The supervision process in counselor education could be studied through microcounseling. The effectiveness of different supervisory styles, the effectiveness of various instructional sequences, and the issue of supervisor congruence with the skill he is teaching could be studied. With the latter, the supervision process could be videotaped and supervisor behavior rated on scales similar to those now used to measure counseling skills. Rand (1969) has suggested that it should be possible to use microtraining to identify the specific skills of the supervisory process. If this is so, a major step could be made toward clarify-ing the nature of the supervisory process.

Carkhuff (1969a, 1969b) argues strongly and effectively for systematic human relations training and presents a useful eclectic model for producing human relations helpers. It has been observed that many of the scales used in microtraining research are closely allied to Carkhuff's facilitative conditions scales. There is need to study the relationship between microtraining and Carkhuff's systematic human relations materials in more detail. It is possible that the behaviors identified in micro-counseling are among those engaged in by Carkhuff's level five (most facilitative) helpers. Thus far, Carkhuff's work has pri-marily focused on judgments of facilitative statements; micro-training may be useful in training helpers and human relations specialists in certain types of facilitative behavior. Further, the microtraining paradigm may be useful in teaching some in-dividuals the broad concepts of facilitative conditions and in further specifying the behavioral aspects of those conditions.

An interesting but as yet untried use of microtraining would be to videotape expert counselors and therapists of differing persuasions and to identify and codify their behaviors. In this way, it may be possible to identify more clearly the similarities and differences of existential, psychoanalytic, behavioral, and other therapists. An examination of Carkhuff's facilitative conditions concepts via microtraining's behavioral emphasis might prove especially fruitful. As an extension of the above, systematic desensitization (Wolpe and Lazarus, 1966) could be studied in detail. While already defined in relatively precise terms, identifying the specific behaviors of desensitization therapy might prove useful in understanding the process more thoroughly and transmitting it to others.

Self-confrontation or seeing yourself as others see you has been identified as the most powerful aspect of the microtraining framework. Berger's (1970) recent book, *Videotape Techniques in Psychiatric Training and Treatment,* explores in detail the importance of self-confrontation via television. However, while the importance of self-confrontation may be agreed to, important questions remain. Why is self-confrontation powerful? What behaviors are most responsive to change under self-observation? What diagnostic categories or what types of patients respond most effectively to self-confrontation? Perhaps the most important and least explored issue in counselor training and therapy is the nature of this ingredient. Microtraining would appear to offer a system wherein the powerful change agent of self-confrontation can be studied via audio or videotape. It seems possible that self-confrontation combines aspects of modeling research of Bandura, important operant dimensions, and issues of the relationship between the observer and his supervisor or therapist. McDonald and Allen (1967) commented that self-observation was most meaningful when tied to specific behaviors which were identified by a warm, trusted supervisor. Their work may provide a basis for more extensive study of the meaning and impact of self-observation in behavior change.

SUMMARY

These suggestions for further research using microtraining and its adaptations are only a sampling of the many ways of using this framework for developing more systematic research procedures in interviewing, dyadic or small-group interaction, and teaching. The structure of microtraining encourages new combinations of interviewing and its practice, of theory and research, and of testing and implementation of new ideas in human research.

The most clearly defined area of microcounseling research at present is in the development of new skills. A relatively specific and workable method of identifying and testing behavioral skills now exists; this method has an important advantage in that the specific skill selected is identified with sufficient clarity that other investigators can examine the same skill to cross-validate results. The specificity of microtraining research should result in clarity of communication in interviewing research which has not often been possible to date.

The effectiveness of the microtraining method has been demonstrated in several studies which illustrate that newly learned skills can be retained and integrated into interviewing practice. However, this seems to be true only if the trainee has the opportunity to practice the learned skills in his daily life or work situation. By analogy, it does little good to give a student a piano lesson which is not followed up by daily practice; similarly, microtraining skills will become integrated only in the context of daily use. There is need to compare the effectiveness of the microtraining paradigm with other models of interviewing training. It is suggested at this time that microtraining represents a model for developing skills best used as a supplement with other models of training.

Finally, the microtraining paradigm provides a laboratory for systematic research and controlled study in many different problem areas of interviewing. While less complex than the interview itself, it is also a more naturalistic setting for study of the variables within the interview. The microtraining paradigm offers a useful framework for a variety of research investigations on the role of models in the interview, the importance of feedback, identifying specific dimensions of verbal interaction between counselor and client, and more clearly specifying important dimensions of the interviewing, counseling, and therapeutic processes.

Chapter Eight

MICROTRAINING: AN OPEN SYSTEM

$\mathbf{M}$ ICROTRAINING PROCEDURES have been presented as a structural and methodological approach to interviewing training. When microtraining as a training structure and the concept of single-skill emphasis is accepted, a wide variety of possibilities become apparent for utilizing this method in vastly different settings and with differing theoretical approaches.

While twelve basic microcounseling skills have been identified, it is hoped that the presentation has been such that these skills serve only as an introduction to the potential for utilizing all or part of the microtraining framework. Teaching interviewing skills is a complex process. Each supervisor or trainer will want to identify his own style, select the skills he considers most important, or develop definitions of new skills.

The structural framework of microtraining provides a systematic method for examining many types of problems in skill training ranging from simple problems of listening to highly complex skills allied with sophisticated theoretical approaches. It is possible to use the same microtraining framework to teach children attending skills or sophisticated therapists complex new methods of handling difficult cases.

The options for using microtraining are many, and this chapter summarizes some of the key structural components of microtraining. This is in the belief that these techniques are only meaningful if they are constantly changed and adapted to meet the individual needs of those who would both teach and learn interviewing and interpersonal skills.

128

THE NECESSARY AND SUFFICIENT CONDITIONS
OF MICROTRAINING

Each individual is unique and responds differently to the several parts of the microtraining paradigm. While many find self-observation of their videotape performance to be the most important aspect of the experience, others find videotape models illustrating how the skill is demonstrated most valuable. Still others consider the written manual defining one specific skill or the assistance of an effective, warm supervisor the most important dimension of their learning interviewing techniques.

Clinical experience has revealed that there is no one way in which microtraining is most effective. Rather, evidence suggests that individuals respond to different aspects of the training paradigm. Some appear to need the support of the written word, others the relationship with an understanding supervisor, while still others apparently could change simply by watching themselves perform without benefit of external influence. As people do indeed differ, the multimedia approach of microtraining appears to be one way in which unique differences can be recognized and utilized for each individual's growth. In the same vein, it may be anticipated that microtraining itself may be an inappropriate vehicle for teaching some individuals intervewing skills. In such cases, alternatives may be considered, ranging from traditional training techniques to in-depth supervisor-trainee relationships such as those proposed by Kell and Mueller (1966) or Wideman (1970). An additional possibility is the combination of microtraining with these powerful relationship approaches.

As noted earlier, McDonald and Allen (1967) in their research noted that different trainees responded most favorably to different parts of microtraining. The same observations were made by Higgins, Ivey, and Uhlemann (1970) examining media therapy. It is suggested that there are no necessary and sufficient conditions for successful microtraining. The question seems to be not which method is best, but *which method, with what individual, under what conditions is best?*

THE IMPORTANCE OF EMPHASIS ON SINGLE SKILLS

Where microtraining has proven ineffective, the inevitable explanation has almost always been that the supervisor or trainee has been unable to focus on a single dimension of the counseling relationship. The supervisor may comment that the trainee had so many errors in his interview that it was necessary to work on more than one problem. A frequent result of such emphasis is that nothing is learned, the trainee is discouraged, and the supervisor is frustrated. We cannot urge too strongly—*in microtraining, teach only one skill at a time.*

It is important to repeat, with additional emphasis, earlier comments on training. It does not seem helpful to try to remake the trainee all at once. When one sees a trainee commiting several errors in one five-minute session, it is tempting to try to rearrange his total performance. When this is tried, failure almost always follows. If a more casual approach is taken, improvement seems to be rapid. ("Don't worry about that error. We are concerned with gradual improvement. Focus on this single dimension.") This is sometimes facilitated by noting instances where the trainee did successfully engage in the skill in his first session and emphasizing this strongly in the supervisory session.

Stoller (1965), in his pioneering work with focused feedback, stresses a similar point. In his therapeutic group work, he emphasizes only one dimension of client behavior at a time, using this as a lever to produce larger changes at a later point. We do not expect therapists to remake a client in one interview, but somehow counselor trainers expect that same miracle from themselves.

Gendlin and Rychlak (1970) explore the issue of teaching single skills and cite the intrinsic reinforcement that comes with learning a new skill. Studies by Bank (1968), Bear (1968), and Lovaas (1968) are examples wherein an individual obtains a sense of confidence and mastery as he learns a new skill. Similarly, we have observed trainees participating in microtraining sessions, who at first lacked self-confidence in their ability to interview, gradually develop increasing confidence as they learn new skills. It might be suggested that one important result of learning a single skill is a generalized feeling of mastery. This sense of mastery in turn results in increased ability to learn and in meaningful individual integration of the skills.

Stressing a single skill and omitting reference to errors in the interview not only results in improvement in the skill in question, but often brings improvement in other areas as well. However, it may be particularly difficult for sophisticated trainees to focus on only one aspect of the interview. It can be helpful to have them specify what they see themselves doing in the interview and then ask them to teach the supervisor their specific skills. The values of such an approach are twofold. First, the supervisor may learn new skills of interviewing, and second, the sophisticated trainee is given an opportunity to look at himself from a new perspective and may learn the importance of the motto, "You don't know what you are doing unless you can teach it to someone else." Another alternative is to present the broad array of available skills and have the trainee select the skill he wants to learn rather than requiring him to learn them in a certain order.

The importance of single skills in microtraining cannot be emphasized too strongly. It is believed that this dimension may be the most important aspect of the entire microtraining framework. Nothing is more discouraging to a beginning interviewer than the feeling that he must be expert in all things simultaneously.

BEHAVIORAL SKILLS AS VIEWED FROM DIFFERENT THEORETICAL PERSPECTIVES

The microtraining paradigm has been consistently presented from an atheoretical model. While some consideration has been made of attending behavior as an underlying theoretical construct, the thrust of this work has been to point out that microtraining is a structural method which can be used by any of a variety of theoretical persuasions to impart their constructs and interviewing strategies. The skills presented here are used with differing emphasis in most models of interviewing. In addition, various theoretical models require the addition of specialized skills and increased emphasis in certain critical areas.

For the employment interviewer or vocational counselor, the

major emphasis may be self-expression skills, such as how to impart information, and paraphrasing skills emphasizing how to help an individual make a decision. Relationship and phenomenological counselors may find reflection and summarization-of-feeling skills most essential in early stages of therapy, but direct, mutual communication with its emphasis on here-and-now interactions may prove more important in later communication. Behavioral psychologists may wish to consider relationship skills as preparatory to involvement in the direction of the interview. Within the microtraining paradigm, it should be possible to develop specialized skills for use in behavior modification. Especially suitable for this purpose is the possibility of conditioning certain verbal response classes in the counseling session.

The specialized techniques of dynamically oriented theories may be clarified through use of microtraining. Techniques used by gestalt therapy with the "hot seat" or in dream interpretation could be taught within a microtraining framework. The use of body cues, important in gestalt therapy, is another feasible area for microtraining. The value of a trainee exploring these powerful techniques under more controlled practice should be apparent. Jungian or Freudian trainees may find interpretation a useful beginning point for developing more sophisticated interpretation skills. An especially difficult interpretation may be role played and a variety of alternative interpretations explored and compared with role models of expert therapists.

Microtraining is not wedded to any one theoretical orientation. Rather, it is a system which can be used in any of a wide variety of different concepts of interviewing training.

TEACHING BEHAVIORAL SKILLS TO CLIENTS

The real frontier in microtraining may well be transferring this method to the classroom, the community mental health center, and the home. If microtraining has proven useful in teaching behavioral skills to counselors, teachers, and a variety of other individuals, the next logical step would be a more extensive exploration of systematic methods of imparting communication skills to people in general.

One could view the skills of interviewing presented here as simply one catalog of skills needed for effective daily interaction. The wife needs not only to attend to her husband but also needs to recognize and listen to his emotions. She should be able to express herself directly and clearly. The child in the classroom can profit from attending and self-expression skills. Early work with mental patients suggests that this complex group also can profit from a behavioral skills approach.

An important question in teaching behavioral skills lies in the genuineness of the encounter. As such, direct, mutual communication, a skill which is not considered learned unless it is forgotten and truly spontaneous, seems essential. Microtraining is only one avenue to teach this skill. Although not generally labeled as such, it has been strongly emphasized in encounter and sensitivity groups. One suggestion for helping individuals communicate more openly and honestly with one another may be an approach which combines some of the advantages of specificity of microtraining with the less easily definable aspects of group work. For example, it may be useful for some individuals to begin the process of behavior change in an encounter group. In the group, skills they lack may be defined and they then may be referred to microtraining to learn these skills. Similarly, some may wish training in communication skills before entering the rigors of an encounter group.

Microtraining in specific communication skills may be a useful addition to school curricula in human relations education. A particular value of microtraining is goal specificity. It tends not to examine individual problems but rather to teach more effective methods through which human beings may communicate with one another. As such, microtraining may prove a useful method of introducing concepts of affective education into the schools.

The do-use-teach model of the behavioral objectives curriculum (Ivey and Rollin, in press) may be useful in a variety of situations where individuals are taught behavioral skills. As noted earlier, in this model, the trainee first demonstrates his ability to engage in a selected behavior, then develops his own way to use the behavior in his daily life, thus facilitating be-

havioral transfer. Finally, the trainee demonstrates his understanding of the skill by teaching it to someone else. The value
of teaching others what you yourself have just learned appears
to be a promising avenue for increasing self-learning and producing a multiplier effect. Many more individuals are exposed to
the concepts than would be possible under traditional models of
instruction. Traditional models focus on cognitive understanding
and rarely even give the individual an opportunity to demonstrate
his ability to engage in the behavior, to say nothing of behavioral
generalization from the immediate situation.

ALTERNATIVES

Microtraining has been presented as a highly specific and
clearly identified method of teaching interviewing skills. The
potential value of this specificity has been continually stressed.
Simultaneously, an effort has been made to show that this framework can be adapted in many ways, that it can be used for a
multitude of purposes, and that it appears to be most effective
when it meets the individual needs and desires of the supervisor
and trainee.

Experience and research has led to the conclusion that
specific commitments to single skills and general adherence to
the microtraining framework leads to the greatest benefit for the
largest number of trainees and clients. This same experience
and research however, has also resulted in an increased awareness of individual differences and the need to adapt any training
program to the needs of the teacher and the learner.

Several varying models for counseling and interviewing training have been presented. They have been complicated by the
suggestion that a major emphasis in training should be with
clients rather than interviewers. The question then becomes,
What commitment to action is most appropriate? The confusion
of the beginning interviewer or the troubled client requires a
commitment to action and action itself. Microtraining represents
one such commitment. Other commitments for interviewing
training such as the Rogerian and analytic models have been
presented. It is not believed that any one model is the *right*

model; rather it seems important that the counselor-trainer commit himself to action in a consistent, integrated manner.

Thus, there are many alternatives for teaching individuals interviewing skills. These range from long-term psychoanalysis to encounter procedures to direct cognitive instruction. The goal of all is to facilitate human development. It is believed that microtraining is simply one more method through which human growth may occur.

BIBLIOGRAPHY

Aldrige, E.: The microtraining paradigm in the instruction of junior high school students in attending behavior. Unpublished paper, Amherst, University of Massachusetts, 1970.

Allen, D. (Ed.): *Micro-teaching: A Description.* Stanford, Stanford Teacher Education Program, 1967.

Allen, D., and Ryan, K.: *Microteaching.* Reading, Addison-Wesley, 1969.

Allen, D.; Ryan, K.; Bush, R., and Cooper, J.: *Teaching Skills for Elementary and Secondary School Teachers.* New York, General Learning, 1969.

Allen, K.; Hart, B.; Buell, J.; Harris, F., and Wolf, M.: Effects of social reinforcement on isolate behavior of a nursery school child. *Child Development,* 35:511, 1964.

Anthony, W., and Carkhuff, R.: The effects of training on rehabilitation counselor trainee functioning. *Rehabilitation Counseling Bulletin,* 13:333-342, 1970.

Appleby, L.: Evaluation of treatment methods for chronic schizophrenia. *Archives of General Psychiatry,* 8:8-21, 1963.

Aubertine, H.: The use of microteaching in training supervising teachers. *High School Journal,* 51:99-106, 1967.

Bandura, A.: Psychotherapy as a learning process. *Psychological Bulletin,* 58:143-159, 1961.

Bandura, A.: *Principles of Behavior Modification.* New York, Holt, 1969.

Bandura, A.; Lipher, D., and Miller, P.: Psychotherapists approach-avoidance reactions to patients' expressions of hostility. *Journal of Consulting Psychology,* 24:1-8, 1960.

Bandura, A., and Walters, R.: *Social Learning and Personality Development.* New York, Holt, 1963.

Bank, P.: Behavior therapy with a boy who had never learned to walk. *Psychotherapy,* 5:150-153, 1968.

Bear, D.: Some remedial uses of the reinforcement contingency. In Shlein, J. (Ed.): *Research in Psychotherapy.* Washington, D. C., American Psychological Association, 1968, Vol. III, pp. 3-20.

Berger, M. (Ed.): *Videotape Techniques in Psychiatric Training and Treatment.* New York, Brunner/Mazel, 1970.

Bergin, A., and Solomon, S.: Correlates of empathic ability in psychotherapy. *American Psychologist,* 18:393, 1963.

Birdwhistell, R.: Some body motion elements accompanying spoken American English. In Thayer, L. (Ed.): *Communication: Concepts and Perspectives.* Washington, D. C., Spartan, 1967.

Blocksma, D., and Porter, E.: A short-term training program in client-centered counseling. *Journal of Consulting Psychology, 11*:55-60, 1947.

Bloom, M.: Personal communication. Indianapolis, University of Indiana, School of Social Work, 1970.

Campbell, D., and Stanley, J.: *Experimental and Quasi-Experimental Designs for Research.* Chicago, Rand-McNally, 1966.

Carkhuff, R.: *Helping and Human Relations.* New York, Holt, 1969a, Vol. I.

Carkhuff, R.: *Helping and Human Relations.* New York, Holt, 1969b, Vol. II.

Carkhuff, R.; Kratochvil, D., and Friel, T.: Effects of professional training: Communication and discrimination of facilitative conditions. *Journal of Counseling Psychology, 15*:68-74, 1968.

Carkhuff, R., and Truax, C.: Training in counseling and psychotherapy: An evaluation of an integrated didactic and experiential approach. *Journal of Consulting Psychology, 29*:333-336, 1965.

Cartwright, R.: Psychotherapeutic process. *Annual Review of Psychology, 19*:387-410, 1968.

Condon, W., and Ogston, W.: Sound film analysis of normal and pathological behavior patterns. *Journal of Nervous and Mental Disease, 143*:338-346, 1966.

Collins, E.: Personal communication. Miami, Dade County Public Schools, 1970.

Cooley, W.: Computer systems guidance. Paper presented to American Educational Research Association Annual Meeting, Chicago, 1968.

Cowles, D.: Personal communication. Greenfield, Massachusetts, Mental Health Center, 1970.

Crowley, T.: The conditionability of positive and negative self-reference emotional affect statements in a counseling type interview. Unpublished dissertation, Amherst, University of Massachusetts, 1970.

Crowley, T., and Ivey, A.: A factor analytic study of communication patterns in media therapy. Unpublished paper, Amherst, University of Massachusetts, 1970.

Danish, S.: Personal communication. Carbondale, Southern Illinois University, 1970.

Deikman, E.: Individual differences in response to a Zen meditation exercise. *Journal of Consulting Psychology, 29*:135-145, 1963.

DiMattia, D.: Personal communication. Amherst, University of Massachusetts, 1970.

Donk, L.: Personal communication. Grand Rapids, Pine Rest Christian Hospital, 1969.

Duncan, S.: Nonverbal communication. *Psychological Bulletin, 72*:118-137, 1969.

Ekstein, R., and Wallerstein, R.: *The Teaching and Learning of Psychotherapy.* New York, Basic Books, 1958.

Exline, R.; Gray, D., and Schuette, D.: Visual behavior in a dyad as affected by interview content and sex of respondent. *Journal of Personality and Social Psychology, 1*:201-209, 1965.

Exline, R., and Winters, L.: Affective relations and mutual glances in dyads. In Tompkins, S., and Izard, C. (Eds.): *Affect, Cognition, and Personality.* New York, Springer, 1965.

Frankel, M.: Videotape modeling and self-confrontation techniques: An evaluation of their effects on counseling behavior. Unpublished dissertation, Rochester, N. Y., University of Rochester, 1970.

Freiband, W., and Rudman, S.: Personal communication. Northampton, Massachusetts, Veterans Administration Hospital, 1970.

Gendlin, E., and Rychlak, J.: Psychotherapeutic processes. In Mussen, P., and Rosenzweig, M. (Eds.): *Annual Review of Psychology.* Palo Alto, Annual Reviews, 1970.

Goldberg, E.: Effects of models and instructions on verbal behavior: An analysis of two factors of the microcounseling paradigm. Unpublished dissertation, Philadelphia, Temple University, 1970.

Greenall, D.: Manpower Counselor Development Program. Unpublished manual. Vancouver, B. C., Canada, Department of Manpower and Immigration, 1969.

Greenspoon, J.: The effect of verbal and non-verbal stimuli on the frequency of members of two verbal response classes. Unpublished dissertation, Bloomington, Indiana University, 1951.

Haase, R.; DiMattia, D., and Guttman, M.: Training of support personnel in human relations skills: A systematic one year follow-up. Unpublished paper, Amherst, University of Massachusetts, 1970.

Haase, R.; Forsyth, D.; Julius, M., and Lee, R.: Client training prior to counseling: An extension of the microcounseling paradigm. Counseling Center Research Report #6, Amherst, University of Massachusetts, 1969.

Haase, R., and DiMattia, D.: The application of the microcounseling paradigm to the training of support personnel in counseling. *Counselor Education and Supervision, 10*:16-22, 1970.

Hackney, H.: Construct reduction of counselor empathy and positive regard: A replication and extension. Unpublished dissertation, Amherst, University of Massachusetts, 1969.

Hackney, R.; Ivey, A., and Oetting, E.: Attending, island and hiatus behavior: A process conception of counselor and client interaction. *Journal of Counseling Psychology, 17*:342-346, 1970.

Heine, R.; Aldrich, C.; Draper, E.; Meuser, M.; Tippett, J., and Trosman, H.: *The Student Physician as Psychotherapist.* Chicago, University of Chicago Press, 1962.

Higgins, W.; Ivey, A., and Uhlemann, M.: Media therapy: A programmed approach to teaching behavioral skills. *Journal of Counseling Psychology, 17*:20-26, 1970.

Hutchcraft, G.: The effects of perceptual modeling techniques in the manipulation of counselor trainee interview behavior. Unpublished dissertation, Bloomington, University of Indiana, 1970.

Irwin, R.: Personal communication. Columbus, Ohio State University, 1970.

Ivey, A.: The intentional individual: A process-outcome view of behavioral psychology. *The Counseling Psychologist,* 1:56-60, 1970.

Ivey, A.: Sharing behavior. Unpublished manual, Amherst, University of Massachusetts, 1970.

Ivey, A., and Hinkle, J.: The transactional classroom. Unpublished paper, Amherst, University of Massachusetts, 1970.

Ivey, A.; Miller, C.; Morrill, W., and Normington, C.: The counselor effectiveness scale. Unpublished report, Fort Collins, Colorado State University, 1967.

Ivey, A.; Moreland, J.; Phillips, J., and Lockhart, J.: Paraphrasing. Unpublished manual, Amherst, University of Massachusetts, 1969.

Ivey, A.; Normington, C.; Miller, C.; Morrill, W., and Haase, R.: Microcounseling and attending behavior: An approach to prepracticum counselor training. *Journal of Counseling Psychology,* 15:II, 1-12, 1968.

Ivey, A., and Rollin, S.: A behavioral objectives curriculum in human relations. *Journal of Teacher Education* (in press).

James, W.: *The Principles of Psychology.* New York, Holt, 1890.

Jones, B.: Guidance and individual planning within a computer-monitored system of individualized instruction for grades 1-12. Paper presented to American Educational Research Association Annual Meeting, Palo Alto, 1968.

Kagan, N.: Personal communication, East Lansing, Michigan State University, 1969.

Kagan, N., and Krathwohl, D.: Studies in human interaction. Research Report No. 20, East Lansing, Michigan State University, Educational Publication Services, 1967.

Kagan, N.; Krathwohl, D., and Farquhar, W.: IPR-interpersonal process recall: Stimulated recall by videotape. Research Report No. 24, East Lansing, Michigan State University, Bureau of Educational Research Services, 1965.

Kagan, N., and Schauble, P.: Affect simulation in interpersonal process recall. *Journal of Counseling Psychology,* 16:309-313, 1969.

Kasamatsu, A., and Hirai, R.: An electronencephalographic study on the Zen meditation (Zazen). *Folio of Psychiatry and Neurology, Japanica,* 20:315-336, 1966.

Keil, E.: The utilization of videotape in job pre-training for mental patients. Unpublished paper, Fort Collins, Colorado State University, 1968.

Kell, B., and Mueller, W.: *Impact and Change: A Study of Counseling Relationships.* New York, Appleton-Century-Crofts, 1966.

Kelley, J.: The use of reinforcement in microcounseling. Unpublished paper, Atlanta, Georgia State University, 1970.

Kennedy, D., and Thompson, I.: Use of reinforcement technique with a first grade boy. *Personnel and Guidance Journal, 46*:366-370, 1967.

Kennedy, J., and Zimmer, J.: A comparison of the reinforcing value of five stimuli conditions and the production of self-reference statements in a quasi-counseling situation. *Journal of Counseling Psychology, 15*:357-362, 1968.

Koestler, A.: *The Act of Creation.* New York, Dell, 1964.

Krumboltz, J.: Changing the behavior of behavior changers. *Counselor Education and Supervision, 6*:222-229, 1967.

Krumboltz, J., and Thoresen, C.: Behavioral Systems Training Program for Counselors. Unpublished paper, Stanford, Stanford University, 1968.

La France, R.: Personal communication. Amherst, University of Massachusetts, 1970.

Levy, L.: *Psychological Interpretation.* New York, Holt, 1963.

Lovaas, O.: Some studies in childhood schizophrenia. In Schlien, J. (Ed.): *Research in Psychotherapy, Vol. III.* Washington, D. C., American Psychological Association, 103-121, 1968.

Luria, A.: The origin and cerebral organization of man's conscious action. Paper presented to the XIX International Congress of Psychology, London, 1969.

Luthe, W.: Autogenic training: Method, research, and application in medicine. *American Journal of Psychotherapy, 17*:174-195, 1963.

McDonald, F., and Allen, D.: Training effects of feedback and modeling procedures on teaching performance. Unpublished report, Stanford, Stanford University, 1967.

Magoon, R., and Golann, S.: Non-traditionally trained women as mental health counselors-psychotherapists. *Personnel and Guidance Journal, 44*:788-793, 1966.

Malamud, D.: The second chance family: A medium for self-directed growth. In Blank, L.; Gottsegen, G., and Gottsegen, M. (Eds.): *Encounter: Confrontations in Self and Interpersonal Awareness.* New York, Macmillan, 1971.

Matarazzo, R.; Phillips, J.; Wiens, A., and Saslow, G.: Learning the art of interviewing: A study of what beginning students do and their patterns of change. *Psychotherapy: Theory, Research and Practice, 2*:49-60, 1965.

Matarazzo, J.; Saslow, G., and Matarazzo, R.: The interaction chronograph as an instrument for objective measurement of interaction patterns during interviews. *Journal of Psychology, 41*:347-367, 1956.

Matarazzo, R.; Wiens, A., and Saslow, G.: Experimentation in the teaching and learning of psychotherapy skills. In Gottschalk, L., and Auerback, A. (Eds.): *Methods of Research in Psychotherapy.* New York, Appleton-Century-Crofts, 1966.

Maupin, E.: Individual differences in response to a Zen meditation exercise. *Journal of Consulting Psychology*, 29:135-145, 1965.

May, R.: *Love and Will*. New York, Norton, 1969.

Mendel, E., and Rapport, S.: Outpatient treatment for chronic schizophrenic patients: Therapeutic consequences of an existential view. *Archives of General Psychiatry*, 8:190-196, 1963.

Miller, C.; Morrill, W.; Ivey, A.; Normington, C., and Uhlemann, M.: Microcounseling: Client's attitudes towards tests. Unpublished paper, Fort Collins, Colorado State University, 1969.

Miller, C.; Morrill, W., and Uhlemann, M.: Microcounseling: An experimental study of pre-practicum training in communicating test results. *Counselor Education and Supervision*, 9:171-177, 1970.

Moreland, J., and Ivey, A.: Interpretation. Unpublished manual, Amherst, University of Massachusetts, 1969.

Moreland, J.; Phillips, J.; Ivey, A., and Lockhart, J.: A study of the microtraining paradigm with beginning clinical psychologists. Unpublished paper, Amherst, University of Massachusetts, 1970.

Murray, E.: The content analysis method of studying psychotherapy. *Psychological Monographs*, 70: (Whole No. 420), 1956.

Norman, D.: *Memory and Attention: An Introduction to Human Information Processing*. New York, Wiley, 1969.

Normington, C.: A comparison of counselor ratings by high school students and experts. Paper presented at the American Personnel and Guidance Association Convention, Las Vegas, 1969.

Patterson, C.: The counseling practicum: An ethical issue. *Counselor Education and Supervision*, 7:322-324, 1968.

Patterson, G., and Guillion, E.: *Child Training: A Manual for Parents*. Rantaul, Rantaul Press, 1968.

Pepyne, E.: The control of interview content through minimal social stimuli. Unpublished dissertation, Amherst, University of Massachusetts, 1968.

Pepyne, E., and Zimmer, J.: Verbal conditioning and the counseling interview. Unpublished paper, Amherst, University of Massachusetts, 1969.

Perlberg, A., and Bryant, D.: Video recording and microteaching techniques to improve engineering instruction. Unpublished paper, Champaign, University of Illinois, 1968.

Perlberg, A.; Peri, J., and Weinreb, M.: Using microteaching techniques and immediate feedback with closed-circuit television to improve teaching in dental education. Unpublished paper, Tel Aviv, Tel Aviv University, 1970.

Phillips, J., and Kanfer, F.: The viability and vicissitudes of behavior therapy. *International Psychiatry Clinics*, 6:75-133, 1969.

Phillips, J.; Lockhart, J., and Moreland, J.: Minimal encourages to talk. Unpublished manual, Amherst, University of Massachusetts, 1969a.

Phillips, J.; Lockhart, J., and Moreland, J.: Open invitation to talk. Unpublished manual, Amherst, University of Massachusetts, 1969b.

Phillips, J., and Matarazzo, R.: Content measures of novices' interview techniques. *International Mental Health Research Newsletter,* 4:11-12, 1962.

Poser, E.: The effects of therapeutic training on group therapeutic outcome. *Journal of Consulting Psychology,* 30:283-289, 1966.

Polanyi, M.: *The Tacit Dimension.* Garden City, Doubleday, 1966.

Quay, H.; Werry, J.; McQueen, M., and Sprague, R.: Remediation of the conduct problem child in the special class setting. *Exceptional Child,* 31:509-515, 1966.

Rand, L.: Personal communication. Athens, Ohio University, 1969.

Reivich, R., and Geertsma, R.: Observational media and psychotherapy training. *Journal of Nervous and Mental Disorders,* 148:310-327, 1969.

Rioch, M.; Elkes, C.; Flint, A.; Usdansky, B.; Newman, R., and Silber, E.: National Institute of Mental Health pilot study in training mental health counselors. *American Journal of Orthopsychiatry,* 33:678-689, 1963.

Rogers, C.: Training individuals in the therapeutic process. In Strother, C. (Ed.): *Psychology and Mental Health.* Washington, D. C., American Psychological Association, 1957.

Rogers, C.: *Freedom to Learn.* Columbus, Merrill, 1969.

Rogers, C.; Gendlin, E.; Kiesler, D., and Truax, C.: *The Therapeutic Relationship and Its Impact.* Madison, University of Wisconsin Press, 1967.

Rogers, J.: Operant conditioning in a quasi-therapy setting. *Journal of Abnormal and Social Psychology,* 60:247-252, 1960.

Rollin, S.: The development and testing of a performance curriculum in human relations. Unpublished dissertation, Amherst, University of Massachusetts, 1970.

Sartre, J.: *Nausea.* New York, New Directions, 1964.

Sartre, J.: *No Exit.* New York, Vintage, 1946.

Scheflen, A.: *Stream and Structure of Communicational Behavior.* Bloomington, University of Indiana Press, 1969.

Schwebel, A.: Personal communication. Columbus, Ohio State University, 1970.

Shor, R.: Three dimensions of hypnotic depth. *International Journal of Clinical and Experimental Hypnosis,* 10:23-38, 1962.

Skinner, B.: *Science and Human Behavior.* New York, Macmillan, 1953.

Stoller, F.: TV and the patient's self-image. *Frontiers of Hospital Psychiatry,* 2:1-2, 1965.

Strupp, H.: *Psychotherapists in Action.* New York, Grune and Stratton, 1960.

Strupp, H.: *Patients View Their Psychotherapy.* Baltimore, Johns Hopkins Press, 1970.

Swets, J., and Kristofferson, A.: Attention. In Mussen, P., and Rosenzweig, M. (Eds.): *Annual Review of Psychology,* Palo Alto, Annual Reviews, 339-366, 1970.

Thielen, T.: The immediate effects of an abbreviated co-counseling supervision approach in teaching empathic skills to counselors-in-training. Unpublished dissertation. Bloomington, Indiana University, 1970.

Trabasso, T., and Bower, G.: *Attention in Learning: Theory and Research.* New York, Wiley, 1968.

Truax, C.: The process of group psychotherapy: Relationships between hypothesized therapeutic conditions and intrapersonal exploration. *Psychological Monographs, 7:* (Whole No. 511), 1961.

Truax, C., and Carkhuff, R.: Experimental manipulation of therapeutic conditions. *Journal of Consulting Psychology, 29:*119-124, 1965a.

Truax, C., and Carkhuff, R.: Personality change in hospitalized mental patients during group psychotherapy as a function of the use of alternate sessions and vicarious therapy pretraining. *Journal of Clinical Psychology, 21:*225-228, 1965b.

Truax, C., and Carkhuff, R.: *Toward Effective Counseling and Psychotherapy: Training and Practice.* Chicago, Aldine, 1967.

Truax, C.; Carkhuff, R., and Kodman, F.: The relationships between therapist offered conditions and patient change in group psychotherapy. *Journal of Clinical Psychology, 21:*327-329, 1965.

Truax, C.; Carkhuff, R.; Wargo, D.; Kodman, F., and Moles, E.: Changes in self concept during group psychotherapy as a function of alternate sessions and vicarious therapy pretraining in institutionalized mental patients and juvenile delinquents. *Journal of Consulting Psychology, 30:*309-314, 1966.

Truax, C., and Wargo, D.: Psychotherapeutic encounters that change behavior: For better or worse. *American Journal of Psychotherapy, 22:*499-520, 1966.

Ullmann, L., and Krasner, L.: *Case Studies in Behavior Modification.* New York, Holt, 1965.

Wahler, R.: Setting generality: Some specific and general effects of child behavior therapy. *Journal of Applied Behavioral Analysis, 2:*239-246, 1969.

Wardwell, E.: Children's reactions to being watched during success and failure. Unpublished dissertation. Ithaca, Cornell University, 1960.

Wawrykow, G.: Video vs. audio feedback in training therapists varying in openness to experience. Unpublished thesis. Waterloo, University of Waterloo, 1970.

Whalen, C.: Effects of a model and instructions on group verbal behaviors. *Journal of Consulting and Clinical Psychology, 33:*509-521, 1969.

Whiteley, J.: Counselor education. *Review of Educational Research, 30:*173-187, 1969.

Whitley, D., and Sulzer, B.: Reducing disruptive behavior through consultation. *Personnel and Guidance Journal, 48:*836-841, 1970.

Wideman, J.: Growth and development in counselor education. Unpublished dissertation. Cambridge, Harvard University, 1970.

Wolberg, L.: *The Technique of Psychotherapy*. New York, Grune and Stratton, 1967, Vol. II.

Wolpe, J., and Lazarus, A.: *Behavior Therapy Techniques*. New York, Pergamon, 1966.

Woodworth, R., and Schlosberg, H.: *Experimental Psychology*, New York, Holt, 1954.

Wrenn, C.: *The Counselor in the Changing World*. Washington, D. C., American Personnel and Guidance Association, 1962.

Zeevi, S.: Microtraining in a community center. Unpublished paper, Amherst, University of Massachusetts, 1970a.

Zeevi, S.: Development and evaluation of a training program in human relations. Unpublished disertation, Amherst, University of Massachusetts, 1970b.

Zimmer, J., and Anderson, S.: Dimensions of positive regard and empathy. *Journal of Counseling Psychology, 15*:417-426, 1968.

Zimmer, J., and Park, P.: Factor analysis of counselor communications. *Journal of Counseling Psychology, 14*:198-203, 1967.

Zimmerman, E., and Zimmerman, J.: The alteration of behavior in a special classroom situation. *Journal of the Experimental Analysis of Behavior, 5*:59-60, 1962.

Zubec, J.: Behavioral and EEG changes after prolonged perceptual deprivation. *Psychonomic Science, 1*:57-58, 1964a.

Zubec, J.: Behavioral changes after prolonged sensory and perceptual deprivation. *Perceptual and Motor Skills, 18*:413-420, 1964b.

Zubec, J.: Effects of prolonged sensory and perceptual deprivation. *British Medical Bulletin, 20*:38-42, 1964c.

Appendix A

MICROCOUNSELING: INTERVIEWING SKILLS MANUAL

INTRODUCTION AND COMMENT ON THEORY

THIS MANUAL PRESENTS twelve skills of interviewing, divided into beginning skills, selective listening skills, self-expression skills, and interpretation skills. Each skill manual is written in a different style; they were not rewritten into one consistent style, as it seemed preferable to present the skills as they were originally developed. It is also expected that those who use microtraining procedures will want to adapt the skills to suit their own needs, and this method provides a maximum number of alternative models.

While the skills presented here grew from inductive experience, there are some considerations which may prove useful in relating them to applied settings. The comments which follow are personal reflections and observations and are designed to stimulate the reader into developing additional modifications in the skills program. Microtraining is most valuable when the individual working with it utilizes the materials in his own style.

Microcounseling is a structural innovation. The microcounseling skeleton can readily be applied to theoretical frameworks as diverse as psychoanalysis, existential psychology, and behaviorism. Further, the single skill concept can be applied without reference to theory in many practical situations. For example, it is possible to use microtraining to identify the counseling skills one needs to interpret tests to employment service applicants or to isolate important dimensions of interaction between the physician and patient in a diagnostic session. As such, microcounseling may be considered atheoretical and a method for examining a wide variety of issues.

However, the twelve skills presented here also represent a content dimension. Through experience we have learned that most counselors find these skills useful regardless of their theoretical orientation or applied setting. For example, open-ended questions, attending behavior, and paraphrasing skills are important to the school counselor, the personnel interviewer, the paraprofessional lay counselor, and the psychiatrist. At the same time, it is recognized that these individuals will use the same skills in different qualitative and quantitative manners. Thus microtraining provides only an introduction to the skill; an individual's theoretical and applied orientation will determine if and how that skill is used.

If there is an underlying theory in microcounseling, it is that microcounseling is a theory about theories. Theories can be viewed simply as differing ways to organize the world of interviewing. It is possible to describe the meaning of the same interview in behavioral, analytic, existential or in any variety of other language systems. Who is to say which description is "right?" There is value and truth in all theory, and theories can be useful as alternative ways to view the world. The best theory is the theory which is most economical in describing what one sees. When considering a complex set of behaviors, the words of psychoanalysis (projection, oedipal complex, etc.) often seem most efficient. However, in developing a treatment plan, behavioral descriptions and methods may be most efficient. Finally, in implementing a treatment plan with another individual, the world of existentialism may provide one with the most helpful way of truly touching another human being.

The several skills of microtraining presented here are important underlying constructs and techniques for work with individuals or groups, but skills training alone does not produce a counselor. It simply gives him a set of behaviors he may draw on when the need is there. Effective interviewers often do not have to think about what they are doing. Skills training such as that provided by microcounseling gives the beginner concrete skills or strategies which are something he can use during his early sessions. For the more experienced individual, microcounseling skills provide a framework from which he can draw interview leads more systematically when an interview does not flow smoothly.

Recent experimentation with microtraining has revealed that having trainees deliberately depict behaviors opposite to that being trained is most useful in facilitating learning. In this way, positive behaviors are seen more clearly. For example, many people attend fairly well and do not become aware of the power and importance of attending behavior until they see what happens when one fails to attend.

Almost all our training in microcounseling is now done in small groups of from six to ten participants. We find that trainees obtain considerable vicarious learning as they watch others participate in the sessions. Individual training seems appropriate for some, but group microtraining sessions will probably grow in importance.

Those who work with microcounseling may wish to modify the basic framework and skills to suit their own views and conceptions of counseling. Microcounseling is first a structural framework for teaching interviewing skills; the specific skills presented here should be viewed as secondary in importance. There are many ways to work to help individuals grow in the interviewing process. Microcounseling and the twelve skills presented here represent one alternative.

THE BASIC SKILLS OF MICROCOUNSELING

Beginning Skills of Interviewing

Most individuals participating in microtraining find it most helpful when they immediately obtain a successful experience. The three beginning skills suggested here are obvious skills to sophisticated trainees but are often eye-openers for the less experienced individual. We have found that simple attending behavior, open-ended questions, and minimal encourages have resulted in trainees feeling more confident about themselves and ready to work on the more advanced and complex levels of interviewing. Those with more sophistication may wish to omit these skills; however, even here it is helpful to see oneself succeeding and to accommodate oneself to self-viewing on video-tape.

In effect, the beginning skills of counseling may give the individual the confidence to grow further. When a person gets confused in the interview, he can always rely on these skills while reorganizing or redirecting the interview. This "fall-back position" gives counseling trainees a sense of capability which frees them to experiment and grow more rapidly.

The three skills presented here are designed to assist the client in talking and helping the client in expressing himself fully. Many beginning counselors or interviewers want to complete the counseling process in one session and thus miss much important data. The emphasis in this section of training is to show the counselor-trainee how he can assist his client to increased awareness. At later points, the counselor can work on helping the client focus his awareness, but in the beginning stages, opening the situation seems most important.

The first modeling tape used with attending behavior consists of a one-minute segment without sound of good eye contact and appropriate body posture. This emphasizes the important nonverbal components of interviewing as a first step toward effective performance. The next segment, again without sound, also one minute in length, presents a negative model with poor posture and little eye contact. A two-minute example then shows a skilled counselor exhibiting good eye contact and posture but poor verbal following behavior. A final two-minute segment demonstrates good posture, eye contact and verbal following behavior.

The modeling tape on open invitation to talk consists of a five-minute interview which includes examples of closed and open questions. With each question, the videotape is stopped and the trainee is asked to identify the question as open or closed and give another example of that type of question. A discussion of closed questions as a focusing technique is also included.

Minimal encourages are presented by a tape of a five-minute interview with a variety of minimal encourages exemplified by a skilled counselor. The trainee is asked to identify these encourages. A negative tape illustrating a wooden, uninvolved posture and a complete lack of encourages is sometimes presented for contrast.

The beginning skills described here can usually be learned in a single one-hour session, although follow-up reinforcement is desirable to help maintain the learned behavior.

Attending Behavior

Good attending behavior demonstrates to the client that you respect him as a person and that you are interested in what he has to say. By utilizing attending behavior to enhance the client's self-respect and to establish a secure atmosphere, the interviewer facilitates free expression of whatever is on the client's mind.

The following are the three primary types of activities which best characterize good attending behavior:

1. The interviewer should be physically relaxed and seated with natural posture. If the interviewer is comfortable, he is better able to listen to the person with whom he is talking. Also, if the interviewer is relaxed physically, his posture and movements will be natural, thus enhancing his own sense of well-being. This sense of comfortableness better enables the interviewer to attend to and to communicate with the client.
2. The interviewer should initiate and maintain eye contact with the interviewee. However, eye contact can be overdone. A varied use of eye contact is most effective, as staring fixedly or with undue intensity usually makes the client uneasy. If you are going to listen to someone, look at them.
3. The final characteristic of good attending behavior is the interviewer's use of comments which follow directly from what the interviewee is saying. By directing one's comments and questions to the topics provided by the client, one not only helps him develop an area of discussion, but reinforces the client's free expression, resulting in more spontaneity and animation in the client's talking.

In summary, the interviewer's goal is to listen attentively and to communicate this attentiveness through a relaxed posture, use of varied eye contact, and verbal responses which indicate to the client that he is attempting to understand what the client is communicating. Specific behaviors which may be utilized are the following:

1. Relax physically; feel the presence of the chair as you are sitting on it. Let your posture be comfortable and your movements natural; for example, if you usually move and gesture a good deal, feel free to do so at this time.
2. Use eye contact by looking at the person with whom you are talking.
3. Follow what the other person is saying by taking your cues from him. Do not jump from subject to subject or interrupt him. If you cannot think of anything to say, go back to something the client said earlier in the conversation and ask him a question about that. There is no need to talk about yourself or your opinions when you are attending.

A final point is to respect yourself and the other person. Ask questions or make comments about things that interest and seem relevant to you. If you are truly interested in what is being said, attending behavior often follows automatically. But remember, the more interested you are, the harder it sometimes becomes to keep yourself quiet and *listen* to the other person.

Open Invitation to Talk

The client comes into an interview with something that he feels is a problem. The initial task of the interviewer is to stay out of the interviewee's way so as to find out how the client sees his situation. Most useful in determining this is the technique of providing limited structure through the use of an open invitation to talk.

An open invitation to talk may be best understood when compared with a closed approach to interviewing. For example,

Open: Could you tell me a little bit about your marriage?
   or

How did you feel about that?
Closed: Are you married? Do you get along with your wife?

It may be observed that the open comments provide *room* for the client to express his real self without the imposed categories of the interviewer. An open comment allows the client an opportunity to explore himself with the support of the interviewer. A closed invitation to talk, on the other hand, often emphasizes factual content as opposed to feelings, demonstrates a lack of interest in what the client has to say, and frequently attacks or puts the client in his place. Closed questions can usually be answered in a few words or with a yes or no.

Crucial to open-ended questions is the concept of who is to lead the interview. While the interviewer does ask questions while using this skill, the questions are centered around concerns of the client rather than around concerns of the interviewer for the client. Questions should be designed to help the client clarify his own problems, rather than provide information for the interviewer. A typical problem with closed questions is that the interviewer leads the client to topics of interest to the interviewer only. Too often an interviewer projects his own theoretical orientation onto the information he is trying to gather, imposes artificial structure too early. If the interviewer relies on closed questions to structure his interview, he is often forced to concentrate so hard on thinking up the next question that he fails to listen to and attend to the client.

Open invitations to talk are extremely useful in a number of different situations. The following are some examples:

1. They help begin an interview. (What would you like to talk about today? How have things been since the last time we talked together?)
2. They help get the interviewee to elaborate on a point. (Could you tell me more about that? How did you feel when that happened?)
3. They help elicit examples of specific behavior so that the interviewer is better able to understand what the interviewee is describing. (Will you give me a specific example? What do you do when you get "depressed?" What

do you mean when you say your father is out of his mind?)
4. They help focus the client's attention on his feelings. (What are you feeling as you're telling me this? How did you feel then?)

Go through the examples above again and give your supervisor some possible closed-ended questions in each case above. Then change your closed questions to open questions.

Minimal Encourages to Talk

Once the client has been helped by the interviewer's attention and open-ended questions to begin telling his story, the interviewer's task is to facilitate his continuing to talk. The interviewer really needs to say very little in order to encourage a client to continue talking, elaborating, and explaining.

Simple "um-hmm's," repetitions of one or two words from what he just said, one-word questions, such as "Then?" are often sufficient. The word "minimal" refers both to how much the interviewer says, which can be very little, and to the amount of direction or intervention he imposes on the content and flow of the interview.

This technique presupposes that the interviewer has tuned in to what the client is discussing. Minimal encourages to talk should follow directly from what the interviewee has just said. When used correctly, the interviewee, although maintaining control of the interview in that he is talking about what he wants to discuss, is forced to elaborate, explain, and to take a more in-depth look at his problem.

Often the interviewer will want and need to talk more and to more actively direct or focus the content of what the client is saying. However, this is an extremely useful technique whether it is used as an adjunct to other techniques or relied on primarily by itself.

More examples of the type of comments described by the title "minimal encourages to talk" are the following:

1. "Oh?" "So?" "Then?" "And?"
2. The repetition of one or two key words.
3. "Tell me more."

4. "How did you feel about that?"
5. "Give me an example."
6. "What does that mean to you?"
7. "Umm-hmmm."

Too many counselors are unaware of the power and importance of minimal encourages. As such, they are unaware of how they may unconsciously influence the direction of interviewing sessions. An understanding of minimal encourages should lead to more self-awareness on the part of the interviewee.

Selective Listening Skills

This section presents four skill manuals dealing with reflection and summarization of feeling and paraphrasing and summarization of content. In addition, a fifth skill, developed in programmed-text form, on selective attention to emotional attitudes toward testing is included. The later skill represents the type of manual that can be developed in special interest areas.

Concepts of reflection of feeling and paraphrasing are presented in the skill manuals as instances of selective attention. We have found that reconceptualizing these common interviewing leads as selective attention to single aspects of the client's communication has been an especially important part of teaching these skills.

We often ask the student to look at our behavior as we talk to him. Then after a short time, we ask him to tell us what we were saying. The content, as he then expresses it, is most often a paraphrase or possibly a summative paraphrase of what we were saying. We next ask the student to tell us what emotions he noted while listening to us and give him the opportunity to give us direct "here and now" expressions of his observations of our emotional states. While this approach sometimes puts the supervisor on the spot, especially if he is not feeling particularly adequate or "together" that day, we have found it invaluable in helping students understand our concepts and in helping them discriminate what we mean when we talk about reflection of feeling as compared to paraphrasing.

Modeling tapes for reflection of feeling have a counselor first

missing obvious feelings, then responding to them more successfully in the later part of the tape. In discussions with student
trainees, an emphasis is placed on selective attention to feeling
states of the client. The modeling tape on summarization of
feeling is about ten minutes in length and includes examples of
both positive and negative summaries.

Paraphrasing modeling tapes have been developed in much
the same fashion as above. In informal discussion with trainees,
we often work with them on using paraphrasing as a method to
sharpen the focus of the interview. The modeling tape on
selective attention to emotional attitudes toward tests follows
the same general framework.

While a two-hour session with three videotaped interviews is
usually required to learn these skills, individuals with more
extensive background learn them more quickly.

Reflection of Feeling

How can you help another person to express the central concerns that he is experiencing? One excellent way is to listen
for and respond to the *feelings* of the client. Try communicating
"I can accurately sense the world as you are feeling and perceiving it," and you can facilitate the client's movement toward more
complete self-awareness and self-understanding.

Being alert to and responding to the *feeling* being expressed,
rather than attending solely to the *content* of what the person
says is the skill with which we are presently concerned. *What*
the client is saying is the *content* portion of the message being
communicated. One must also listen to *how* the client says what
he does. For example, the client may speak more quickly when
communicating enthusiasm, more slowly when communicating
discouragement, etc. It is this *feeling* portion of the communication to which you are to pay particular attention.

Being alert to and responding to the feeling being expressed
is a skill which is appropriate at *any* time, regardless of the
nature of the feeling (positive, negative, or ambivalent) and
regardless of the direction of expression (toward self, others,
the counselor and counseling situation, etc.).

In the examples below, you will have an opportunity to select the alternative which indicates that you understand the client's attitude, the situation as it appears to the client—the alternative which if spoken to the client would most likely evoke a response of, "That's right!"

EXAMPLE 1

"So I'm wondering if you can help me to find a new major" . . . (pause) "I suppose if I did find one, I'd just bungle things again. . . ."

a. Are you sure that it is necessary to leave the major you are now in?

b. You feel that it's pretty futile to try again.

c. What majors have you been considering?

In the first example, responses a and c seek additional information from the client, without giving adequate recognition to client feelings. Response b accurately reflects the feeling being expressed.

EXAMPLE 2

"What do you think I ought to do—jump off a bridge, or look for another college to flunk out of?"

a. There just doesn't seem to be any way out!

b. Have you applied to other schools?

c. Have you thought about trying a junior college where there would be a little less competition?

In this example, response a accurately reflects the client's feeling, whereas responses b and c provide suggestions as to what the client might do, without giving adequate recognition to the feeling of discouragement which the client is experiencing.

EXAMPLE 3

"You know, it's a funny thing, but when I go in for an oral quiz, I just feel shaky all over! It's the silliest thing! Why should I do that?"

a. Are you an anxious person in many situations?

b. How shaky do you become?

c. This reaction puzzles and concerns you!

Here, responses a and b seek additional information, whereas in response c, the gist of the client's expression is caught and rephrased in fresh words.

Some behaviors you may want to try are the following:

1. Listening for feeling. Remember that *what* the client is saying is only part of the message being communicated to you. *How* he says what he says is extremely important. A change in breathing or in the speed of talk, a sigh, a blush, a stammer, an extra emphasis upon a particular word—any of these can be important cues as to feelings of the client. Words which communicate emotions and feelings should be noted.

2. Timing your comments. Do not try to respond to every comment by the client. You may simply want to smile, nod, say "Mm-hmm," etc., until there is an occasional opportunity to reflect feelings of the client.

3. Reflecting feeling. As you listen for and find instances of client expression of feeling, reflect this feeling by restating what the client is experiencing in your own words. If the client should say, "I wish I could talk to my dad about things like this, but I never seem to get up the nerve," you might respond, "You are a little bit afraid of your dad?"

   Your goal is to understand what the client is experiencing, and to communicate to the client that *"I am with you*—I can accurately sense the world as you are feeling and perceiving it."

Paraphrasing

Paraphrasing achieves three purposes. These are (a) to convey to the client that you are with him, that you are trying to understand what he is saying, (b) to crystallize a client's comments by repeating what he has said in a more concise manner, and (c) to check the interviewer's own perceptions to make sure he really does understand what the client is describing.

Just as the reflection of feeling involves some reiteration of content, paraphrasing entails some recognition of the client's feeling. The primary difference is one of emphasis. The first concentrates on the emotional aspect of the cilent's communication, while the latter emphasizes the cognitive or content aspect of the message.

When utilizing this technique, the interviewer attempts to feed back to the client the essence of what the client has just said. Used in this manner, this skill is extremely functional in clarifying confusing content, tying a number of recent comments together, highlighting issues by stating them more concisely, and checking one's perceptions.

The following are some good examples of accurate paraphrasing:

Client: I don't know about him. One moment he's nice as can be, and the next he is a real bastard.

Interviewer: He's pretty inconsistent then.

Client: Every day there is something new to do. There must be ten different activities going on at any one time around here.

Interviewer: So there are lots of activities for you to choose from.

Client: He's really crumby. His degree is from a non-accredited school, he's had very little training, and he has a very poor relationship with his wife.

Interviewer: You don't think he is very competent.

Client: He is supposed to be an authority, yet he's mixed up all the time. He talks as if everything he says is true, but he's quite uncertain a lot of the time.

Interviewer: You feel that if a man gives you the impression that he knows everything, then he should know everything.

With your supervisor, go back through the list above and develop inappropriate paraphrases which might tend to lead the client off on a new, perhaps irrelevant path. Then change your inappropriate paraphrases back into a more suitable form.

Summarization of Feeling

When an interviewer uses summarization, he attempts to recapitulate, to condense, and then clarify what the client has said. As such, a summarization of feeling is very similar to a reflection of feeling with one major exception—a summary of feeling covers a longer time period and involves a broad range of feelings which the client has expressed.

Thus, instead of noting only one or two immediate feelings, the interviewer notes the overarching emotional dimensions expressed by the client and then summarizes them in a meaningful form for him. A summary which integrates the emotional aspects of what the client has been discussing serves at least three functions. These are as follows:

1. It may crystallize what the interviewee has been talking about. By noting emotional undertones expressed throughout the interview, you help the client focus on the issues which concern him most.
2. It may serve as a stimulus for further talk on the issue. This conversation itself may be deeper and more meaningful to the client if you have "tuned in" to his emotions.
3. Simply summarizing what you think you have heard often helps you find out whether or not you are perceiving the client correctly.

A summarization of feeling expressed well and fitting the client's needs is one of your most powerful tools to convey to the client that you are with him, have empathy, and can understand how it feels to be in his shoes. As such, it may help you to think deeply about what the client is feeling, attend to his diverse emotions, and attempt to experience them yourself. Then pull back, sort out what you see, separate yourself from what seems objectively true and summarize for the client what you sense. This is an important way to communicate to another human being that you understand him and are with him.

Specific behaviors you may wish to engage in are as follows:

1. Use reflections of feeling to indicate to the client that you are with him. Selective attention to feelings will assist him in exploring his emotional states.
2. Note consistent patterns of emotion as he progresses through the interview. Also note his inconsistencies or polarities of feelings. Most clients have mixed feelings toward important love objects or situations, and showing

the client how he has expressed his mixed feelings may be especially valuable to him.

3. At two or three points during the session and at the close of the session restate in your own words, the feelings and perceptions that the client has been communicating.

Summarization of Content

When an interviewer uses summarization, he attempts to recapitulate, to condense, and to crystallize the essence of what the interviewee has said. While a summary thus resembles a paraphrase, it differs in one fundamental respect—the temporal period covered by a summary is substantially longer than that of a paraphrase. The latter deals with the client's last few sentences or a short paragraph. A summary puts together a number of client paragraphs, or an entire phase of a session, or may cover even an entire interview.

A summary integrates cognitive elements of what the client has been discussing and serves at least these three major functions:

1. It may crystallize in a more coherent and integrated manner what the interviewee has been talking about. It may help him put facts together.
2. It may serve as a stimulus for further exploration of a particular topic or area.
3. Because it pulls together materials discussed over a substantial period of time, it frequently serves as a necessary perception check for the interviewer.

Summarizations are frequently used in any of the following situations (this is not an inclusive list):

1. When the interviewer wishes to structure the beginning of a session by recalling the high points of a previous interview.
2. When the interviewee's presentation of a topic has been either very confusing or just plain lengthy and rambling.
3. When an interviewee has seemingly expressed everything of importance to him on a particular topic.

4. When plans for the next steps to be taken require mutual assessment and agreement on what has been learned so far.
5. When, at the end of a session, the interviewer wishes to emphasize what has been learned within it, perhaps in order to give an assignment to the client for the interval until the next session.

Behaviors you may want to engage in include the following:

1. Using paraphrases and open questions to help the client keep talking.
2. Giving special attention to central threads of information throughout the session. For example, when the client talks about a decision he is to make, note the main issues he is considering so you can give them back to him later.
3. At several points during the session, timing your comments appropriately and summarizing for the client what you have heard him say. Your selective summary is effective if it prompts him to talk in a deeper fashion or helps him to clarify his own thinking.

Learning Client's Attitudes Toward Tests: A Specialized Skill

1.1   How can we help another person understand and use information from standardized tests? The first step in communicating test information is to understand how the client feels toward the test and testing in general. Unless we can obtain some idea about how the person feels about tests, helping him use test information is a most difficult task.

1.2   Before we discuss test results with a client, we should learn how the client_____about the test.

1.3   The correct answer is *feels*. We need to learn and understand the client's attitudes and emotional feelings toward tests before we attempt to interpret test results.

1.4   How can one learn and understand how another feels about tests? First, let us explore your attitude toward tests. Do you like tests? Do they make you nervous? Do you find them a stimulating experience? Do you recall some key experiences when you took ability tests? What did they mean to you? List below some of your own emotional attitudes and feelings toward tests.

_____

_____

_____

1.5 You should have listed words such as "good experience," "I was scared," "tests bug me." Here we are looking to see if your general attitude toward tests and feelings about tests can be brought to your awareness.

1.6 How can one learn about and understand the attitudes which a student has toward tests? In a short time, you will talk with a student who may have taken a number of guidance tests including ability or IQ tests, vocational interest tests, and personality tests. We want you to learn how he (a) felt about the tests he has taken and (b) feels about guidance or psychological tests in general.

1.7 There are three key ideas to keep in mind as you learn the skill of understanding how a student feels about tests:

a. Relax physically and *center your attention on the client.* We find that counselors are most effective and enjoy themselves most when they forget about themselves and center on the other person.

2. Secondly, *use eye contact* to help you focus on the other person, and to communicate to the other person that you are listening. You need not gaze fixedly or intensely. At times you may want to look at the person as you talk, at times you may glance down as you think about something the other person is saying, and then return your gaze, etc.

c. Thirdly, and most important, set for yourself the task of *following* what the other person is saying. Be selective in your following and relate to the other person's comments on the topic of attitudes toward tests.

1.8 The three key factors enabling the understanding of another person are:

a._____ b._____ c._____

1.9 The correct answers are *focus your attention on the client, maintain eye contact,* and *follow* what he says.

1.10   Now to prepare specifically for your session with the student. We will first introduce you to your client. We want you to begin the first sessions as follows:

"Here are samples of guidance tests which you may have taken. How do you feel about the guidance tests which you have taken?"

1.11   After that question, you should *follow* the client and pay particular attention to his attitudes and feelings toward tests. For example, the client may say, "It was kind of fun to take that test." A good counselor response emphasizing attitude would be:

"You enjoy taking tests?"
     or
"What about the test did you like?"
     or
"Do you usually enjoy taking tests?"

Poor responses might be:

"How long did it take you to finish the test?"
     or
"What kind of test did you think it was?"
     or
"What year are you in college?"

Each of the good responses focused on the attitudes of the client toward the test or other tests and *followed* what was just said by the client. The poorer responses actually change the topic discussed and ignore any emotional aspects of the client's response.
1.12   The client says, "I was somewhat nervous during the test." A good counselor response might be:

a. "The test was hard?"
b. "What other test have you taken lately?"
c. "Tests kind of bother you?"

1.13   The correct answer is "c." It is the only response which discussed emotional attitudes or feelings. The other two items center on facts such as the difficulty of the test and ideas not really related to what the client was just saying.
1.14   Before you see your client, we wish to go over the skill

of listening carefully for client attitudes and feelings toward tests once again.

The first and most important suggestion is to forget yourself and *focus entirely on the client.* Look at him and listen to him . . . he will give you cues and ideas on how to respond. You do not have to look inside yourself for new topics.

The second suggestion is that you pay attention to the *emotional aspects* of the client's comments about tests. Do not discuss how tests are made, their limitations, etc. You want to focus on how the client *feels* about tests.

Thirdly, always *follow* what the client says with a comment on your part related to what he just said. Do not topic jump or introduce your own ideas.

1.15   To understand what a client feels about tests, one should forget about oneself and_____on the client's attitudes and emotions.

In this study, the counselor should pay particular attention to the_____a client has toward tests.

A counselor should not topic jump, but should_____ the client's last comment about tests.

1.16   focus, center; feelings; follow

1.17   You should now be ready to begin your first session with a client and discuss emotional attitudes toward tests.

Skills of Self-Expression

If an individual is to listen to others effectively, it is helpful if one is able to listen to himself and express himself clearly. We have found that training in expression of feeling is invaluable in helping beginning counselors learn what feelings are; this in turn seems to make them much more able to recognize and be in touch with the feelings of their clients. The modeling tape for expression of feeling shows an individual first expressing content, then later expressing emotion about the same topic. Usually a one-hour session is sufficient to teach this skill.

The skill of direct, mutual communication is a complex set of skills and closely resembles the feedback and sharing typical of the sensitivity training session. We may note here that the manual is a short programmed text integrated with specific video models. Sessions using this program have always been exciting and challenging, and the depth of communication between participants has been impressive. When using this set of materials with students, one should be especially aware of ethical considerations. The modeling tapes have been taken from actual depth encounters between two individuals and are shown to represent the possible communication that can occur between two people that truly work on their communication processes. Developing these modeling tapes may prove to be the most difficult task of the entire program. Two hours is required to teach this skill. However it may also be taught without the physical presence of a supervisor. In such cases, however, a supervisor should be close at hand to assist with any complications which may arise.

The concept of sharing behavior is still in the formative stage, but it has shown considerable promise to help individuals express themselves more easily and completely. We have found that the concepts demonstrated in this manual have proven useful to individuals through simply helping them tell a client some important information or in helping a shy individual make a presentation before a group. Sharing behavior is a skill which can be taught to people in general rather than to only counselors. However, certain shy or quiet counselors may profit from work in this area. The modeling tape simply portrays positive and negative examples of the specific behavior in question. Time to teach this skill varies with the individuals' needs.

Expression of Feeling

Unless one understands one's own self, it is extremely difficult to understand others. One important dimension of self-understanding is the ability to attend and to express one's own emotions or feelings. This training skill is focused on helping you express your emotions more clearly and sharing them with others.

Those who enter counseling training may find that the ability to express their own emotions facilitates their progress in counseling. Individuals unable to express emotions often cannot recognize them in others. While theorists differ on whether the counselor should express his feelings in the interview, all agree that awareness of one's own feelings is crucial in the counseling process.

The skill training you will receive will focus on helping you express your feelings to another individual. We would like to help you learn two things. First, you should learn the difference between expressing *content* (what you are saying to the other) and second, the *expression of feelings* (the emotional experiences you have about what you are saying). Many, perhaps most, people attend solely to the content of their words and are not aware of their underlying emotions.

The following examples illustrate the difference between expression of content and expression of feeling (the *italicized* words represent feeling states):

1. I went to John Jay High School and took mathematics, English and art. (Expression of content.)
   When I went to high school, I *hated* it. Mathematics was a *drag;* the English teacher *bugged* me; and art was the *only good thing* during the day. (Expression of feeling.)

2. How do I *feel?* Well, I *feel* I am an *interesting* person. I have traveled a lot. I have seen the world. I *feel* I know a lot about what is going on. (Expression of content.)
   How do I *feel?* I *feel* pretty *good* about myself. I've been around a lot and from what I've seen, I am *happy* to be me. Whenever I look around me I *feel* that I'm *lucky,* that I have been able to *enjoy* myself. On the other hand, maybe I am a little *arrogant,* and that makes me *wonder* about myself sometimes. (Expression of feeling.)

3. I *feel* like things haven't been going right lately. The cat died, my therapist raised his rates, and my wife just got a job. (Expression of content.)
   I really *feel depressed.* The first thing that *got me down* was when my cat died. I felt so *sad* I sat down and *cried.* Then my *damn* therapist raised his rates and didn't even *care* enough to tell me; that really made me *angry* and then when I told him about the cat he didn't react and I *felt really crumby.* Then my wife up and gets a job with-

out telling me; somehow I feel she just doesn't *care* about me at all and it makes me *sad, sad, sad.* (Expression of feeling.)

When one talks about any situation, he can talk about his feelings or the content of what happens. Your task today is to talk about your emotions rather than about facts.

You may wish to take the following topics and discuss them briefly with your supervisor, first demonstrating an expression of content, then demonstrating an expression of feeling: School, family, sports, an accident, a childhood experience.

In summary, move inside yourself, look at your emotions. While words provide basic clues in this skill, also think about your nonverbal communication. If you talk about sad things, do you look sad? If you talk about happy things, do you look happy? As you learn to express feelings, put your body and words together and really attend to your emotions. In this way, you can best understand yourself.

Sharing Behavior

How can one communicate one's ideas and feelings to another person, a small group, or a classroom of children? One important skill of communication is sharing behavior, a set of specific behaviors which will result in your developing better means of communicating yourself and your ideas to others.

Sharing behavior is structured in a similar fashion to attending behavior. First, if one is to share himself with others, he must be *physically relaxed* and in tune with his own body. Second, eye contact with the other individual is important, but *psychological eye contact should be with the self.* This may sound a bit bizarre, but we are suggesting that you look at others but focus your attention within yourself. Finally, *verbally follow yourself.* Simply let yourself take the lead, ideally talk about something that interests you. If you follow these three simple directions, you can find yourself "turning on" and getting more enthused about what you are talking about.

An example occurred when I was to make a presentation to an important audience and felt myself awkward, tense, and stumbling over my words. I thought to myself of the concepts of sharing behavior. I realized I was paying so much attention to the audience that I was forgetting myself as a person. I believed in what I had to say. How could I put it across? I deliberately relaxed to put myself together (it could be observed easily by anyone in the audience) and took a deep breath. I deliberately put my thoughts in myself and started talking about what I cared about. For a short time it was awkward, but soon I forgot that I had engaged in deliberate behaviors and was "turned on" and "turning on" the audience.

Observe the better speakers and most interesting people in your surroundings. You will find that they use some variation of this simple theme. Turn on a television set and observe the individuals you see; it is sometimes helpful to view the set with the sound turned off.

However, sharing behavior in extreme forms can result in an individual talking so incessantly that he is unable to see the reactions he is obtaining from others. Sharing behavior does not necessarily represent a perfect way to express oneself. Sharing behavior is only a part of effective self-expression but essential before communication at higher levels of expression can occur.

Sharing behavior has been found most helpful in working with individuals who claim they have "nothing to talk about" or who have difficulty in expressing their ideas. It is considered a beginning skill which may give some individuals their first success in self-expression in a considerable period of time. It has proven useful to the individual who finds it difficult to stay on the topic.

One example where this skill was used successfully was with a depressed patient who only talked about himself; through use of this skill he learned to stay on other topics and talk about issues beyond himself. Similarly, this skill can be used to help salesmen express themselves more clearly, a boy express himself more clearly to his teacher, and in a variety of other situations. It is especially useful to those who have difficulty in expressing themselves before groups.

In summary, when engaging in sharing behavior, do the following:

1. Relax physically, put your feet on the floor. Assume a position of decisiveness. Do not sit back in a retiring position. You are to express yourself.
2. Use eye contact, but keep your primary attention within yourself. Look at your audience physically, but keep your main focus on your own thoughts and ideas.
3. Talk on one topic and stay on that topic. Do not let your thoughts wander. It helps if you talk about something you like to talk about. If you care and express yourself well, others will soon listen. Paint a picture with words.

Direct, Mutual Communication

1.1   This is a program in interpersonal relations designed to help you communicate with your partner. Its purpose is twofold —to teach basic material concerning human relations and to provide an opportunity for actually experiencing a new kind of interaction with others, rather than just talking about it.

1.2   The conversation you just had fits into one of the three following patterns. Read the patterns below one at a time and decide which most accurately fits the conversation you just had. The answer will tell you which conversational pattern usually occurs under these circumstances. Refer to the answer *after* you together have decided which description fits your conversation best.

a. There was tendency to talk about topics such as politics, religion, etc., which do not directly concern your personal feelings about each other.
b. You both talked about things that were quite important to your *feelings about* and *relationship with* each other. You could see clearly some of your partner's *real feelings* about you and your relationship.
c. Either one or both of you talked about things that were important to your relationship, but you found it *difficult to understand one another* about these issues.

1.3   The most effective type of interpersonal communication is "b." You have probably discovered from this experience that there are certain things which can be predicted about most conversations between people. Most people tend to talk during conversations whenever they can. They tend to show agreement for the sake of good will.

When people know one another thoroughly, they often attempt to discuss things of more importance, but they are frequently unable to understand *one another's* feelings about the issues discussed as in example "c."

1.4   You can help your partner get the most from this program if you keep in mind that he is a person with feelings. It is important to become aware of just what his_____are.

1.5   feelings

1.6   People begin to relate at a more meaningful level when they are able to *share* their *inner feelings* and *experiences* with the other. As a person begins to allow another to enter his world of feelings and experiences, he becomes more real and genuine. Generally, he gets more meaningful and intimate responses from the other person, and the relationship deepens.

WATCH THE TAPE as two girls talk.

What is the result of Pat's (the girl on your left) sharing her feelings with Karen?

1.7   Karen is moved by Pat's sharing and comments on her specific reactions to the experience. Pat is then able to respond to this feedback from Karen, letting Karen know how she receives this. As the tape ends, Karen is just about to share something of herself. She has attended to Pat's feelings before responding with her own. In short, Karen has said to Pat:

a. I hear what you have said.
b. It makes me feel this about you.
c. I want to add this to what you have said.

This simple procedure is what we would like you to attempt today.

1.8   WATCH THE TAPE again as two men, Max and Bill, interact. Note especially what happens when Bill shares an inner experience with Max.

1.9   Bill's sharing of his experience with statistics prompts Max to respond to him, letting Bill know how Max has received this new information about Bill, and then Max gives Bill important feedback. Max says that he would like to be able to "tell you something like that." Bill now knows that when with Max, it's OK to share deep feelings and that this sharing makes Max feel closer to him.

Again, the following pattern is used:

a. I hear you saying.
b. It makes me feel this way.
c. I want to add this.

It is exactly the same as it was for Pat and Karen.

When you and your partner interact, *try to share your inner experiences.*

1.10 An even more significant sharing that a person can have with another is the feelings they have toward one another, both in the past and right now in the present. The focus in such cases is on the interaction between the two people and their sharing of feelings about each other.

In the tapes which follow, the partners attempt to discuss their relationships with each other. The first tape shows two girls discussing their problems of relating to each other at the *present moment.*

WATCH THE TAPE.

1.11 Note that J., the girl on your right, discussed F.'s reaction to an earlier statement ("I like you."). She then attempts to share her reactions to other situations when she is faced with praise from another. The pair discuss the immediate problems of talking meaningfully in the room. J. now understands more about F.'s difficulties in relating to her.

When you interact, try to discuss the feelings you have about each other.

1.12 The next tape that you will see will focus on interactions which occur in the immediate present, IN THE ROOM. Max and Bill are communicating their immediate responses and reactions to each other. We feel that this is a deep and meaningful way of interacting. As the tape begins, they are discussing a past interaction, a situation in which Max had asked Bill whether Bill found him to be "sickening."

WATCH THE TAPE as Max and Bill respond to their immediate feelings about each other.

1.13   Max has asked Bill for feedback. Bill gives his reactions to Max, and lets Max know exactly how he was feeling about him. Max then lets Bill know that such feedback is welcome and has reduced the tension in Max. From Max's reactions, Bill can also conclude that it is safe to respond to Max in an open way, i.e. sharing immediate feelings.

When you interact, share your reactions to your partner. 1.14   You will soon interact with your partner in another five-minute session. As you interact in this next session, *try to focus on your immediate feelings and impressions of your partner* and share them with him.

Remember the following points:

a.   Hear what he says.
b.   Tell him how it makes you feel about him (or it).
c.   Add what you wish to add in the way of feedback.

It will be about ten minutes before your second videotaped session. You may talk informally with your partner about whatever you wish until that time.

❖   ❖   ❖

2.1   You have just completed your second interaction. Take time now to review with your partner what has taken place between you. Let the following sections guide this discussion. 2.2   Which of the three patterns discussed in section 1.2 of the first training section most clearly marked your interaction this session?

a.   There was a tendency to talk about *topics* such as politics, religion, etc. which do not directly concern your personal feelings about each other.
b.   You both talked about things that were quite important to your *feelings about* and *relationship with* each other. You *could see clearly* some of your partner's *real feelings* about you and your relationship.
c.   Either one or both of you talked about things that were important to your relationship, but you found it *difficult to understand one another's feelings* about these issues.

2.3   Hopefully, your interaction was more marked by inter-actions like those in "b." You should be sharing personal feelings with your partner and responding to him with your reactions to and feelings about him.

If your interaction was not marked by "b," then discuss with your partner what you were doing in the past session. Perhaps you were still afraid to share these feelings with him. If this is so, perhaps you could discuss with him some of the uncom-fortable feelings you had about sharing feelings with him.

2.4   Did you feel that your partner was hearing what you had had to say? Discuss this with him.

2.5   Did you let your partner know how you felt about what he had to say. Discuss this with him.

2.6   Were you able to do the following:

   a.   maintain eye contact?
   b.   maintain physical attention?
   c.   listen to the *feelings* of your partner?

2.7   At this point, we would like you to review two of the models that you have already seen. Section 2.7 refers to the first model and section 2.8 to the second model which you will see.

Tell the operator when you are ready to review the models. As you watch the tape, compare your past interaction to the ones on the tape.

2.8   Bill's sharing of his experience with statistics prompts Max to respond to him, letting Bill know how Max has received this new information about Bill, and then Max gives Bill im-portant feedback. Max says that he'd like to be able to "tell you something like that." Bill now knows that when with Max, it's OK to share deep feelings and that this sharing makes Max feel closer to him.

Again note the following pattern:

   a.   I hear you saying.
   b.   It makes me feel this way.
   c.   I want to add this.

2.9   The next tape that you will see will focus on interactions which occur in the immediate present, IN THE ROOM. Max and Bill are communicating their immediate responses and reactions to each other. We feel that this is a deep and meaningful way of interacting. As the tape begins, they are discussing a past interaction, a situation in which Max had asked Bill whether he (Max) was too nice. (Max had asked whether Bill found him to be "sickening.")

WATCH THE TAPE as Max and Bill respond to their immediate feelings about each other.

2.10 Discuss areas in which you and your partner need to improve in order to attain the communication level shared by Max and Bill.

2.11 As you interact with your partner in this next session, try to share your feelings with him and respond with your *reactions* (*feelings*) to him.

Remember the following:

a. Hear him and let him know that you hear him.
b. Share your inner responses and feelings with him.
c. Share or add something of yourself with him.

2.12 You will have a few minutes before your next videotaped session. Talk about whatever you wish until you are told to begin your next videotaped session.

Interpretation

To date, only one general interpretation skill has been developed. However, it should be possible to develop a variety of interpretive skills focusing on different theoretical persuasions. One can imagine the value to a student trainee of seeing expert therapists of differing persuasions responding to similar client information.

It is suggested that interpretation skills are central to the more advanced therapist, interviewer, or counselor. There is need to develop additional and more specific skills of interpretation.

The modeling tape presenting interpretation is longer than others, being fifteen minutes in length. Several examples of alternative interpretations and their effectiveness are presented. Training in interpretation skills usually involves two hours, although more sophisticated trainees may show proficiency after one hour.

While all skills work well when used with small class groups, interpretation provides an unusually good opportunity for student trainees to apply their theoretical data to the same client and see the results demonstrated. The group can then discuss among themselves and with their supervisor the quality of the several interpretative styles that they used.

Interpretation Manual

While interpretations may vary in content, depending upon the theoretical orientation from which they are drawn, they all have one element in common. When an interviewer makes an interpretation, he is presenting the client with a new frame of reference through which the client can view his problem and, hopefully, better understand and deal with his situation. Seen in this light, an interpretation is not too dissimilar from either a paraphrase or a reflection of feeling.

One function of both the paraphrase and the reflection of feeling is to crystallize for the client either the content or the feeling component of what he has just said. The interviewer remains, for the most part, within the client's *own* frame of reference. However, in an interpretation, the interviewer provides the client with a *new*, more functional frame of reference.

The accuracy of a feeling reflection or a paraphrase is gauged by the client's verbal and nonverbal reaction to it. Likewise, one criterion for the accuracy of a single interpretation is whether or not the client can utilize it to more effectively cope with his problem, both emotionally and intellectually. Another criterion for the validity of an interpretation is the interviewer's own personal comfort with his view of the client's world. If the interviewer is not congruent with himself and the client, the interpretation is less likely to be accepted.

The following are examples of interpretation as compared with a reflection of feeling or paraphrase:

Client (who has a record of absenteeism): I really feel badly about missing so much work.

Interviewer: You're really troubled and worried. (Reflection of feeling.) You've been missing a lot of work. (Paraphrase.)

You've missed a lot of work and you are aware of how the company views absenteeism. This gives you concern as to where you stand. (Interpretation.)

Client (with agitation): My wife and I had a fight last night after watching a sexually exciting movie. I tried to make love and she rejected me again.

Therapist: You're upset and troubled. (Reflection of feeling.) Your fight followed a sexually exciting movie. (Paraphrase.) The movie stimulated you sexually and you sought to make love to your wife even though you have said you expect her to reject you. (Interpretation.)

You've mentioned several times you are interested in making love with your wife after some external stimulation. You've never mentioned your wife as being sexually exciting. (Interpretation.)

The feelings of rejection trouble you. Are these feelings similar to the feeling you mentioned in the dream last week? (Interpretation.)

In each example, the interviewer takes some part of the essence of what the client has said (both intellectually and emotionally) and summarizes it for the client, adding other data which the interviewer considers relevant. There are a multitude of responses possible in any client utterance.

Interpretation has traditionally been viewed as mystical activity in which the interviewer reaches into the depths of the client's personality and provides him with new insight. However, when one conceives of an interpretation as merely a new frame of reference, the concept of depth becomes less formidable. Viewed in this light, the depth of a given interpretation refers to the magnitude of the discrepancy between the frame of reference from which the client is operating and the frame of reference supplied by the interviewer. For example, a client may report a dream in which a seedling he planted grew into a tree and was mysteriously cut down. The interviewer could make a number of interpretations which vary in terms of their depth:

1. You lost something you really worked hard for.
2. Your life has had a number of disappointments.

3. You are very unsure of your successes.
4. You are afraid of losing your penis.

Interpretations will vary with the theoretical orientation of the interviewer. You may wish to go back over the situations described in this manual and interpret them from varying theoretical perspectives with your supervisor. We are suggesting that the successful therapist has many alternative interpretations available to him. He selects his interpretations in relation to the immediate and long-term needs of his client. If an interpretation is unsuccessful, he uses this new data to develop another, more meaningful response.

ALTERNATIVE METHODS FOR ORGANIZATION OF MICROCOUNSELING LABORATORIES IN INTERVIEWING COURSES

The outline of skills suggested on the preceeding pages is one impression of how interviewing training might be organized. While it is the basic structure and conceptual framework behind our training in interviewing methods, it should be pointed out that we seldom follow the sequence suggested. Instead, we find when we are working with individuals with differing levels of skill and varying interests, it is preferable to constantly adapt the order of teaching skills. We also adapt the method which we use in teaching them and frequently omit or add skills to an individual's program.

There is no one right way to teach counseling skills. Individuals differ. Some prefer the structured presentation of skills suggested in this manual. Others may learn most effectively by choosing their own skills, using some of these plus developing others. We have seriously considered the possibility of establishing a counseling-skills laboratory in which students are introduced to the skills available and the method of developing them and then are allowed to implement their own self-instructional programs in small groups. Setting up this type of skills training requires space, well-organized materials, and equipment but may prove to be an important tool for helping individuals grow on their own.

Microteaching procedures are most effective when used individually or in groups of up to six (possibly eight) individuals. Those interested in microtraining will want to experiment with both individual and group training. It is suggested that individual microteaching be tried first, for it is easy to lose direction in a group unless one is thoroughly familar with microteaching procedures. The importance of teaching only one skill at a time cannot be stressed enough.

While the standard microtraining procedure of counsel-training-recounsel has been found most effective, it is clearly not the only way to teach single skills of interviewing. We recommend using the standard framework to teach trainees at least two skills. In this way, the important dimensions of experiential learning, modeling, instructions, feedback, and supervision are experienced by both the trainer and the trainees. It is then possible to change the framework as all participants have a common base from which they may move. This is the recommended procedure, although other adaptations of microtraining can be made and are outlined in the accompanying text in detail. What seems most important is an organized framework to teach skills and to enable individuals to grow.

One might develop many alternative organizations, modifications, and additions in developing a course of interviewing. The following are a few suggestions.

1. The instructor of an interviewing course in eclectic interviewing procedures may want to follow the outline suggested in the manual. He may wish to examine each skill from differing theoretical foundations. It should prove interesting to have beginning counselors actually discover significantly different uses of the same skill by those of varying theoretical persuasions. For example, the behavioral counselor may use reflection-of-feeling statements, but his purpose is to selectively reinforce client statements, and his later methods vary considerably from the existentially oriented therapist.

2. When working with paraprofessionals or less sophisticated groups, attending behavior and the beginning skills of counseling should be introduced first. Before moving to selective listening, expression of feeling and perhaps other self-expression skills

should be developed in the trainee. It is sometimes difficult to teach selective listening skills to an individual who cannot listen to himself.

3. When using this framework to teach a behavioral orientation to counseling, the manuals can be rewritten to include more of the jargon (reinforce, shape, etc.) of behavior modification. Attending behavior and the beginning skills of counseling seem important, as do selective listening skills. The selective listening skills would best be presented as selective reinforcement, and trainees might practice skills of shaping verbal topics in the counseling session. For example, it is possible to teach trainees to reinforce emotional statements about a narrow topic, then to extinguish this response class, and finally to shape a new class of responses in the client. Additional skills of behavior modification such as relaxation training and desensitization procedures could be developed into a microtraining program.

4. Phenomenologically oriented therapists may wish to rewrite the manuals in another direction, making them less behavioral with more emphasis on experiencing the client. It would be anticipated that skills of reflection and summarization of feeling, as well as direct, mutual communication and adaptations of interpretive skills would be most appropriate in this theoretical orientation. One might anticipate that the teaching of skills in a phenomenological orientation would be more "person-centered" and the skills themselves would be viewed as vehicles to help the supervisor and trainee relate more effectively and grow in a more mutual manner.

5. Those of dynamic orientation will find some of the skills useful in helping the beginning therapist orient himself to the interview. However, the bulk of training would be in interpretive skills. There is need for development of a wide variety of skills relating specifically to dynamically oriented therapists. It is believed that microteaching might prove useful as a method to make more specific the methods and systems of dynamic psychology. It is also recognized that most of those with strong dynamic orientations and many of those with existential leanings may not favor microteaching methods.

6. Interviewing training for business employment or per-

sonnel counseling would probably focus on attending skills, paraphrasing and focusing for decision making, and extensions of self-expression skills. One important self-expression skill might be presentation of data concerning a company or job. Another would seem to be centered on interpreting tests. Depending on the orientation of the course, reflection of feeling and interpretative skills might be less or more important. Skill manuals could be rewritten in places with examples focusing on the specific situations encountered by the trainees.

7. A leaderless laboratory could be established for the teaching of skills. Students in groups of six to eight would meet weekly with the agreement that they would train themselves in the skills. Modeling tapes of skills would be available to them, as well as consultant support. Evidence is that if the skills are clearly defined, trainees may be able to teach themselves skills without the need for constant supervision. Some graduate students have commented that their most valuable training in interviewing comes from discussion with other students. The leaderless laboratory simply provides a more formal structure. Another alternative would be for advanced students to supervise beginning students in microtraining, thus providing experiences for new students and supervisory experience for advanced students.

8. Microtraining skills may be used in short intensive workshops of from one to five days. In such workshops, specialized problems such as handling specific types of cases. evaluating personnel decisions, or even sales training methods could be examined in some depth. Such workshops could also be used to train supervisors in microcounseling procedures; trained individuals do not need the full complement of skills, and short workshops could provide a basic understanding of the methods and concepts of microtraining.

9. Microcounseling could also be used as a supplement to interviewing courses. It is not necessary that the full complement of skills be taught; certain specific skills relevant to the specific phase of the course could be integrated into the course plan. Similarly, microtraining laboratories can be added on to existing course structures as a supplementary credit experience.

These are but a few examples of course approaches to the microtraining skills. Basically, they may be summarized by stating that the instructor has to determine his goals for the course or laboratory, organize the skills in the way he feels most appropriate, and add or delete skills as seems appropriate. While we recommend using the standard microtraining paradigm as a beginning point, many adaptations and modifications of the framework may be employed. Microtraining procedures apparently may be taught as effectively in groups as they may be taught individually.

It is anticipated that this manual would be most suitable for beginning graduate courses in counseling and clinical psychology, school guidance, social work training, and general interviewing courses. However, others have found these skills useful with medical interns, psychiatric trainees, speech therapists, sales training, undergraduate courses in education and psychology, and in client training in community recreation or mental health centers.

COUNSELOR EFFECTIVENESS SCALE

The Counselor Effectiveness Scale (CES) has been used frequently in microtraining research and many requests for the scale have been received. Therefore, the scales and data on its development are included in this manual.

The CES has been primarily used to measure client attitudes toward their counselor. When used in evaluating the counselor before and after microtraining sessions, it has proven to be a sensitive and useful instrument. However, we have also found the instrument to be highly reactive to changes in the client's environment and thus do not recommend its use in other than immediate pretraining and posttraining microcounseling sessions. However, when using large samples, this reactivity may be of less importance.

The report on the development of the CES written by the author, Dean Miller, Weston Morrill, Cheryl Normington, and Richard Haase follows.

Item Selection

Ninety-three items of the semantic-differential type (adjective continua) were randomly ordered in a semantic-differential format and comprised the initial item pool. Estimates of item reliability and validity were obtained in the following manner: two graduate psychology classes (N=30) were asked to rate two videotaped models of counselors, with one model portraying desirable counselor behavior and the second portraying undesirable or ineffective techniques. Means, standard deviations, standard errors, and confidence limits (.05 and .01) were computed for every item on each of the two models. The standard error of each item served as a measure of its reliability, while the difference between confidence limits of the positive and the negative models served as a measure of validity of that item. The standard errors and confidence limits of every item were graphically plotted, and item selection for the final scales was completed by analyzing and selecting items which represented the most optimal combination of the two. Items were judged on the degree that they had low standard error (reflecting high agreement among raters) and a wide separation between confidence limits for the positive versus the negative model (a representation of that item's ability to discriminate). Two parallel forms of 25 items each were constructed on this basis.

Reliability

Parallel form reliability (coefficient of equivalence) was computed between form 1 and form 2 of the scale and yielded a value of +.975, which is significant beyond the .001 level of confidence. Raters consisted of students enrolled in a psychological testing course (N=18) and who had no previous experience with either a semantic differential format or the scale under consideration. For all practical intents and purposes, they could be considered "naive" raters.

Inter-rater reliability was computed using Kendall's Coefficient of Concordance. Kendall's W allows one to obtain a measure of agreement between k judges who have made N

observations. This obviated the need to compute $\frac{N(N-1)}{2}$ combinations of coefficients between individual judges and then
proceeding to average these.

Undergraduate student raters (N=7) were utilized as judges
and were asked to rate a videotape model of counseling on 50
observations made by these judges on the semantic differential
format (25 on form 1 and 25 on form 2). Kendall's W was
applied to these 50 observations and yielded a value of +.37,
which is significant far beyond the .001 level of confidence. In
essence, we now have information which indicates that all seven
judges are utilizing essentially the same criteria of judgment.
Hence, we are assured of significant inter-rater reliability of
this scale.

Validity

The use of two radically different models of counselors allowed
for a test of validity of the two scales by means of their ability
to discriminate between rationally defined good model and
rationally defined bad model of counselor behavior. The degree
to which the scales can discriminate between these two models
allows one to estimate the validity of the scales (i.e. whether the
scale is actually able to measure or discriminate between effective
and ineffective counselors). Undergraduate student ratings of
both models (N=18) were obtained for both form 1 and form 2
of the scale. Means, standard deviations, and *t* values were
computed. The results of the test of significance of the difference
between mean ratings of model 1 and model 2 are presented in
Table 1.

TABLE 1

SIGNIFICANCE OF THE DIFFERENCE BETWEEN MODEL 1 AND
MODEL 2 AS RATED ON EACH OF TWO PARALLEL FORMS
OF A SCALE TO MEASURE COUNSELOR EFFECTIVENESS

Form	d.f.	Mean of Model		t	p
		1	2		
1	17	66.25	131.22	8.28	.001
2	17	65.00	134.44	10.60	.001

The results of the significance of the difference between the
two models as measured by the forms of the scale under con-

sideration are indeed encouraging. The fact that the items were originally drawn by a technique that utilized the same two models may indicate that further validity studies should be designed which utilize different counselors in different situations. Further work in this area shall be implemented.

Conclusions

It appears, at least tentatively, that the scale under consideration to measure counselor effectiveness is a promisingly reliable and valid instrument in short-term situations. It therefore seems tenable to apply this scale to experimental work. Further reliability and validity data on the scale, per se, is recommended.

Rating Scale of Counselor Effectiveness
Scale #1

sensitive ___:___:___:___:___:___:___	insensitive
relevant ___:___:___:___:___:___:___	irrelevant
nervous ___:___:___:___:___:___:___	calm
confident ___:___:___:___:___:___:___	hesitant
skilled ___:___:___:___:___:___:___	unskilled
attentive ___:___:___:___:___:___:___	unattentive
comfortable ___:___:___:___:___:___:___	uncomfortable
interesting ___:___:___:___:___:___:___	dull
confused ___:___:___:___:___:___:___	sensible
confident ___:___:___:___:___:___:___	doubts his ability
gloomy ___:___:___:___:___:___:___	cheerful
calm ___:___:___:___:___:___:___	jittery
intelligent ___:___:___:___:___:___:___	unintelligent
irresponsible ___:___:___:___:___:___:___	responsible
sincere ___:___:___:___:___:___:___	insincere
apathetic ___:___:___:___:___:___:___	enthusiastic
tense ___:___:___:___:___:___:___	relaxed
colorful ___:___:___:___:___:___:___	colorless
boring ___:___:___:___:___:___:___	interesting
formed ___:___:___:___:___:___:___	formless
unreal ___:___:___:___:___:___:___	real
sociable ___:___:___:___:___:___:___	unsociable
shallow ___:___:___:___:___:___:___	deep
careless ___:___:___:___:___:___:___	careful
polite ___:___:___:___:___:___:___	rude

Rating Scale of Counselor Effectiveness
Scale #2

skillful	___:___:___:___:___:___:___	clumsy
competent	___:___:___:___:___:___:___	incompetent
confusing	___:___:___:___:___:___:___	clear
meaningful	___:___:___:___:___:___:___	not meaningful
deep	___:___:___:___:___:___:___	shallow
sympathetic	___:___:___:___:___:___:___	unsympathetic
close	___:___:___:___:___:___:___	distant
socially inept	___:___:___:___:___:___:___	socially adept
decisive	___:___:___:___:___:___:___	indecisive
friendly	___:___:___:___:___:___:___	hostile
realistic	___:___:___:___:___:___:___	unrealistic
irritable	___:___:___:___:___:___:___	pleasant
passive	___:___:___:___:___:___:___	active
insecure	___:___:___:___:___:___:___	secure
strong	___:___:___:___:___:___:___	weak
nice	___:___:___:___:___:___:___	awful
erratic	___:___:___:___:___:___:___	stable
consistent	___:___:___:___:___:___:___	inconsistent
indifferent	___:___:___:___:___:___:___	conscientious
lazy	___:___:___:___:___:___:___	industrious
mature	___:___:___:___:___:___:___	immature
inattentive	___:___:___:___:___:___:___	attentive
social	___:___:___:___:___:___:___	anti-social
efficient	___:___:___:___:___:___:___	inefficient

Appendix B

TYPESCRIPT OF PREATTENDING AND POSTATTENDING BEHAVIOR SESSIONS

T HE FOLLOWING TYPESCRIPTS were completed as part of Edward Aldrige's doctoral dissertation at the University of Massachusetts. In this study, Aldrige was concerned with teaching junior high school students basic listening skills. It may be observed in the first five-minute session that the student serving a listening or "counseling" role frequently interrupts, changes the topic of discussion, and portrays poor listening skills. Following attending behavior training, positive verbal following behavior may be observed. The trainee constantly stays on the topic, talks considerably less and presents a picture of a person able to listen effectively.

It may be observed that the qualities inherent in poor listening skills are characteristic of counselors who are less effective. We have chosen this sample of pretraining and posttraining sessions because (a) it is a particularly vivid example of attending and non-attending behavior and (b) it illustrates the potential value of teaching listening skills to those who do not necessarily interview or counsel. Finally, it should be observed that we are not concerned with the topic actually discussed when teaching attending behavior but with simply helping the trainee stay on a single line of conversation.

PRETRAINING SESSION

Counselor: What are you planning to do when you get out of school? Ah what college do you like? -

Counselee: I don't have, I haven't given it really much thought— I really don't know what I want yet.

Counselor: I haven't really thought about it too much either.

Counselee: Well it's not too early to start thinking, but I don't know. I'm thinking I might like to be a drama major, but I'm not sure.

Counselor: Isn't that . . . uh, I don't know, you can't really make that much money from drama can you? Anyway not too much?

Counselee: No! It's not so much the money, I like to act. (Stammers.) I don't know how good I am but I like to act.

Counselor: I like to act too, but people tell me that I'm good but I think I'm a ham so I wouldn't like to put people on. I hate to watch bad acting so I don't want people to have to watch the same thing.

Counselee: (Laughs.) We were thinking of writing Woody Allen, he's uh the writer of a play I'm in and see if he'd kinda like . . .

Counselor: (Interrupts.) He's a comedian!

Counselee: Woody Allen, yeah! I'm not sure . . . he's basically a writer I think! But . . . our set . . . for the play, it's beautiful. You have to come and see it. It cost two hundred dollars and it's very nice.

Counselor: Is Woody Allen uh any relation to_____Allen?

Counselee: (Clearing throat.) I don't know.

Counselor: Do you know_____Allen?

Counselee: No I don't know_____Allen! (Slight irritation noted.)

Counselor: Well . . .

Counselee: (Interrupts.) Why, is she in school?

Counselor: No I don't think so. I think she (was) in my other school. I don't know why I asked you. (Sighs.)

Counselee: We have one of the ambassador's mothers [reference to the play] helping, Rory_____he's in . . .

Counselor: (Interrupts.) Roy's a mother?

Counselee: Rory's mother! (Slight irritation noted in voice.)

Counselor: Oh, Rory's mother!

Counselee: Yeah! She's a professional . . . worked in theater. She offered to . . . to help us. She's done most of the work on our set.

Counselor: Uhm, is she a good artist?

Counselee: Yes, very good! She uh made the seal over our—you know—the bald eagle with the arrows and the ivy or whatever it is.

Counselor: Bald eagles! There's not that many left now. They're extinct now?

Counselee: Naw! (Laughs.) I'm talking about the seal. You know, like on the president's seal, it's above uh the desk. It's really beautiful. She's a good, a good uh artist. Mr. _____ is the director.

Counselor: Oh, I didn't know, he's a French teacher isn't he?

Counselee: Right! He's good. I had him last year.

Counselor: (Long pause—no response.)

Counselee: How do you think you're doing in math?

Counselor: Yeuch!

Counselee: Really! Well listen, on the first report card I got I didn't do so well. Matter of fact I got mostly "C's" but then I got my second report card.

Counselor: I don't understand any of this math stuff about squares or anything even though I'm doing OK on the tests. Yeuch!

Counselee: (Amused tone.) You understand it.

Counselor: Well . . . it's possible.

Counselee: What do you do during the summer?

Counselor: Mmm oh all sorts of . . . not much really.

Counselee: Do you travel, or do you stay at home?

Counselor: My mother's going to get a job. What about you? (Faintly mumbled.)

Counselee: Well, let's see, we have this summer place up in _____, New Hampshire. It's in the family—and we have a hill and there's about four cottages on it.

Counselor: Do you uh, own all the cottages?

Counselee: Well, it's in the family. My father doesn't own all of them. We own a lot of land and uh . . .

Counselor: (Interrupts.) We're thinking about buying a house but we haven't got the money yet.

Counselee: (Ignores interruption and continues.) It's a nice quiet place. And then there's this, uh, road that's blocked off during the summer, so it's nice and quiet. And across the street from this road there's this lake. Then we have a stretch of beach and two canoes, three actually. One leaks quite badly.

Counselor: Did you ever tip over?

Counselee: Yeah! (Irritated acknowledgment.) One time my cousin and I and a friend of his were in their canoe. We'd gone down the river which leads into the center of town. Once we, uh, when I was first learning how to. . . . I carried two people and two dogs.

Counselor: (Interrupts.) In a canoe?

Counselee: Yeah! But we were only about . . . it was only a flat lake so . . .

Counselor: (Interrupts.) They don't have any round lakes?

Counselee: They don't have any round lake; mostly flat lakes!

Counselor: Well, rivers?

Counselee: Yeah, OK! But as I was saying, he was in a rush to get back because his mother said you'll have to be back by five o'clock or else! (Laughs.) So we were sprinting across the middle of the lake and this wise guy in a motor boat comes around and swamps us!

The five-minute session ends.

POSTTRAINING SESSION

Counselor: You were saying something about your cottages?

Counselee: Oh yes—this nice quiet place. Also I, I fly during the summer. I take flying lessons. Where we live there's an airport, it's for light aircraft. Ah, I, uh, don't fly during the winter, during the school year, but I fly during the summer.

Counselor: Ooh lucky! (Pleasing, eager note to voice.)

Counselee: Yeah. I, I, I don't know how I got interested in it but somehow I did. Now I have my mother taking flying lessons and I nearly, we almost bought a plane but we couldn't make ends meet.

Counselor: That's too bad, it would've been fun.

Counselee: Yeah, it would be. You could take trips that you couldn't take, you know, just by driving. And this summer

I'm painting a house in order to get money for it also.

Counselor: For the plane or for flying?

Counselee: For flying lessons.

Counselor: What do you do when you fly—I mean do you fly the plane?

Counselee: Uh huh! Well, it's hard to explain. But, ah, well first of all, on your first flight you learn what the basic controls are. Like the rudder pedals . . . they affect the yaw, and the planes ailerons, and, uh, the (control) wheel turns them. That way, if you turn it, you'll roll back. If you push the (control) wheel forward you go down, if you pull it back you go up. That's what you learn—when to coordinate. You have to learn to coordinate the controls. Otherwise if you just use the pedals when you go into a turn, you go like this (uses hands to illustrate) and it's not good.

Counselor: Did you ever do that?

Counselee: Yes, I did when I first started out but not now.

Counselor: Is it scary?

Counselee: No it isn't. Well after you do it right it isn't. First time I did , ah, a steep bank, I, I went a little too steep. And you know how in the war movies you see the planes slide off like that (illustrates), that's what I did.

*Counselor*s Good! (Faintly but encouragingly expressed.)

Counselee: It was, ah, kinda funny because my instructor was sitting there in the back seat. He was sitting there like this (illustrated posture) and whistling, like uh he wasn't in the plane and this wasn't happening to him. It was funny!

Counselor: Gosh, wasn't he scared?

Counselee: He should've been!

Counselor: How many years have you been doing this, flying like that?

Counselee: Well last, last year was my first year.

Counselor: And when do you get a license?

Counselee: Not until you're seventeen. (Laughs.)

Counselor: When will you be seventeen?

Counselee: About two years from now.

Counselor: You're only fifteen? Mmm you look bigger?

Counselee: (Pleasant jocular tone.) Well I'm a precocious kid you see. And, ah let's see, sometime this year I'll turn 16 and I'll be able to solo. It means I can fly alone without anyone in the plane.

Counselor: Without a license?

Counselee: No, a license means I can take other people up in flight. But I can't do that now unless they know how to fly themselves, then, they, then I can take em!

Counselor: How far along is your mother (in learning to fly)?

Counselee: Ah, not very far, just a couple of hours. She doesn't have that much time to, ah, develop it yet. So she's going to wait till this summertime to take it up then. My father, I'm going to work on him a little bit more.

Counselor: Think you'll get him?

Counselee: Yeah, think I'll get him! I know he likes it . . . so it's a pretty sure thing.

Counselor: The flying family. (Pleasant voice.)

Counselee: Yeah, right!

Counselor: (Laughs.)

Counselee: My sister, ah she's renting a horse this summer, for a hundred and fifty dollars for two—for one month. She's a horse bug.

Counselor: How about you?

Counselee: No, I've already tried but I don't really like it. I got off the saddle and felt like I was about to split right down the middle.

Counselor: I've never ridden, so I don't know. (Given in an acknowledging, encouraging voice.)

Counselee: Well, it's lottsa fun. It was funny, one time I wasn't there and my sister was telling me about this. We have an Austrian kid who uh comes over from ah Austria to America for the summer, for the past two or three summers. And he and my sister go riding together. One time they were going through, ah, going through the woods on a (bridle) trail and they stepped, one of the horses, stepped on a rotten piece of wood and out came all these bees. And so Deitrich, that's the name of this Austrian kid, Deitrich's horse sat right down and he was about to get off. Then all of a sudden (the horse) stood up and galloped away and you know he's holding onto the saddle for dear life. It must've been a comic sight.

The five-minute session ends with both laughing.

Appendix C

EXAMPLES OF RECENT RESEARCH IN MICROTRAINING

THREE DOCTORAL DISSERTATIONS completed at the University of Massachusetts in June, 1971, provide useful supplemental data concerning the validity of the microtraining model. Aldrige examined behavioral count data stemming from the training of junior high school students in attending behavior. Sadker demonstrated the transfer of learned behavior in microtraining to the classroom setting. Moreland, in a controlled study of traditional psychiatric training compared with microcounseling, has demonstrated the effectiveness of microtraining.

These studies offer helpful conceptual frameworks for conducting microtraining research and together suggest new directions for further testing of the model.

BEHAVIORAL COUNTS IN MICROTRAINING RESEARCH

Much of the research in microtraining has relied on generalized ratings on five point scales of specified counselor behaviors. While reliability has been satisfactory on these scales, more precise measures were desired. As research and training in microcounseling has progressed, it has become increasingly apparent that it is possible to count specific behaviors and avoid the subjectivity of the five-point scales, despite their early usefulness.

Aldrige was concerned with teaching the skill of attending behavior to junior high school students. While clinical experience indicated that this counseling skill could be easily taught to students and that it was valuable to them in interpersonal experience, data was needed to prove experimentally that younger people could learn counseling skills.

191

Sixteen junior high students were randomly divided into a microtraining group and a placebo group which received no specific training. The eight experimental subjects received the usual microtraining instructions in attending behavior with the exception that the written manual was adapted and changed to focus on interpersonal communication and everyday life. It is believed that the listening skills of attending behavior are useful in many interpersonal interactions beyond those previously studied in counseling training.

Through a carefully designed eight-hour training program for two independent raters, Aldrige received .90 or better inter-rater agreement on behavioral counts on such items as number of eye-contact breaks, number of arm and hand movements, and number of topic changes, the latter taken from a typescript. His findings comparing the trained and untrained groups are summarized below:

NONVERBAL AND VERBAL BEHAVIORAL COUNTS

Variable	Group	Pretest Mean	Posttest Mean	Significance Level
No. of breaks in eye contact	E	14.75	3.00	.01
	C	17.06	15.13	
No. of arm and hand movements	E	9.94	7.06	N.S.
	C	9.25	6.44	
No. of leg and foot movements	E	5.88	1.88	.05
	C	3.13	3.56	
% of talk time for counselor	E	52.06	30.88	.01
	C	46.09	50.07	
Mean length of utterance of counselor	E	10.27	7.87	N.S.
	C	9.88	13.60	
No. of topic changes initiated	E	7.63	2.00	.01
by counselor	C	6.75	5.50	

It may be observed that the students who received microtraining experience had fewer eye-contact breaks, less bodily movement, less speaking time during the interview, and less frequent topic changes. In addition, the students trained in listening skills were rated as more effective by those whom they interviewed.

Particularly important in Aldrige's study is the demonstration that microcounseling skills need not be reserved solely for counselor trainees but may also be taught to people in general. One belief and recommendation of this book has been that counseling skills are general communication skills and as such should not be restricted to a small group of professionals but made available to pupils as part of their regular educational experience. Aldrige has used similar training programs with disturbed children and family communication problems. His clinical experience has been that training in such skills has been highly facilitative to family interaction.

Also valuable in this study is Aldrige's demonstration, in specific behavioral terms, of both verbal and nonverbal changes in the behavior of the trainee. Previous data had indicated that this was so, but the behavior counts in this study suggest that it is possible for increasingly precise work and study within the microcounseling framework.

INTEGRATION OF MICROTRAINING WITH A TOKEN ECONOMY

Sadker was interested in teaching elementary school children ". . . a skill which occurs infrequently in the classroom—the skill of student-initiated, higher-order questioning." This skill demands that students ask their teachers for more than facts (Who was president during the Civil War?). Higher-order questions demand evaluation, problem-solving, seeking cause-and-effect relationship, comparisons, and divergent open-ended thinking. Examples of higher-order questions would include "What were the causes of the Civil War?" "What might have happened if Lincoln had not been assassinated?" "How did Grant show he was an effective general?" It may be observed that higher-order questioning is a variant of the open-ended questions used within the microcounseling framework.

Sadker points out that much student behavior in our schools is passive and fact-centered and that up to 85 percent of student-teacher interaction is teacher initiated. The purpose of instruction in higher-order questioning was to assist elementary children in developing a more initiating and conceptual approach to classroom work.

The subjects for the study were eight fifth-grade students. Four received instruction in the behavior of higher-order questioning, while the remainder did not. The teacher in this class was unaware of the purpose of the study. Selected students were trained in the skill with the traditional microtraining framework. After higher-order questioning had increased in microtraining to a predetermined criterion level, a token economy was established in which students were awarded points for asking appropriate questions. The points could be exchanged for various toys and games in a "store."

Thirty-two experimental sessions were conducted. Frequency counts of higher-order questions within experimental and control subjects were made by two raters stationed in the classroom. Inter-rater reliability was computed at .97. Raters also noted the teacher's response to these questions and inter-rater reliability for teacher consequation was .95. Five experimental phases were conducted: baseline, microteaching, reinforcement I, no consequation, and reinforcement II. No reinforcement in the form of points for questions was provided in the baseline, microteaching, or no-consequation phases.

The table below presents the mean higher-order questions per five-minute interval for each phase of the study for trained and untrained students:

MEAN HIGHER-ORDER QUESTIONS PER FIVE-MINUTE INTERVAL
PER PHASE FOR TRAINED AND UNTRAINED STUDENTS

Students	Baseline	Microtraining	Reinforcement I	No consequation	Reinforcement II
Trained Students					
A.	.20	.35	1.02	.18	1.01
B.	.02	.08	.61	.06	.82
P.	0.00	0.00	.46	0.00	.42
A.	0.00	0.00	.38	.03	.28
Untrained Students					
M.	.28	.07	.05	.17	.17
A.	0.00	0.00	.09	.08	0.00
B.	.02	.07	0.00	0.00	.05
P.	.02	.04	.01	0.00	.07

Sadker also developed individual operant charts for each of the eight students during the 32 sessions which provide dramatic pictures of the effectiveness of the training and the importance of the token reinforcement to help maintain the learned behavior. Sadker also found it possible to categorize systematically the type of higher-order questions asked by the students. Problem-solving and cause-and-effect questions were asked most frequently.

During the experiment, 242 higher-order questions were asked by the eight students and only two of these failed to receive consequation by the teacher. Generally the teacher answered the question without evaluating the pupil statement. Only five questions received praise from the teacher ("good question"), while 15 were evaded or received a reprimand. Increased positive reinforcement from the teacher might have increased the number of higher-order questions and even perhaps maintained these questions during the period of no token reinforcement. It may be observed that the teacher required all students to raise their hands before speaking. The teacher's control over the lesson demanded that students would have to really work to initiate questions. This, coupled with the relative lack of positive reinforcement for higher-order questions, helps explain the return to baseline responding during the no-consequation phase of the study.

Sadker's work has implications for interviewing training and for microcounseling research. Perhaps most important among these is the importance of environmental reinforcement of learned behavior if new skills are to be retained. Training may not be helpful in teaching skills of interviewing unless the work environment provides the interviewer with a chance to try learned skills and actually rewards interviewing-type behavior. If the rewards on the job center on correctly filling out forms, it may be anticipated that learned counseling behaviors and skills will not be maintained. Further, unless the trainee can use the learned skills in a real interview and finds them facilitating his interaction, he will not continue to use them.

MICROCOUNSELING AS COMPARED WITH TRADITIONAL
PSYCHIATRIC TRAINING

Moreland studied 24 second-year medical students at the University of Oregon Medical School who were also enrolled in an introductory psychiatry course. The major question being asked was the effectivenes of microtraining as compared to more traditional efforts. Randomly assigning 12 subjects to each group, Moreland gave one group training with six skills of microcounseling (attending behavior, open-ended questions, minimal encourages, paraphrasing, reflection of feeling, and summarization) while the remainder received regular individual-didactic training.

The major criterion for interviewing effectiveness was evaluation of interviews conducted by trainees with outpatients pretraining and posttraining. Four patients were interviewed by three experimental and three control trainees both before and after the training provided. Ten minutes of each pretraining and posttraining interview were videotaped for later analysis. Tapes were randomly intermixed, and two trained judges rated them on a variety of scales.

The results showed that both groups significantly improved their interviewing skills. The microcounseling group, however, improved more on the attending-behavior rating scale and on the number of reflections of feeling and open-ended questions. The microcounseling group also scored more favorably on the Therapist Error Check List in which the quality of individual statements are rated. A series of five-point Carkhuff-Truax-type scales revealed no significant difference in ratings between the groups.

Moreland points out that of 22 dependent variables, the microcounseling group improved on 20 of them, while the control group improved on 11. These data are especially important, as this study represents the first attempt to systematically compare microcounseling with traditional training in an applied setting. Prior research with microcounseling has been more of a laboratory nature and has not considered the integration of several skills used in actual therapy sessions. It seems apparent that learned behavior within microcounseling does generalize.

Of course, maintenance of that learned behavior will depend on further practice and reinforcement in the applied setting.

Moreland also found it possible to categorize each statement in the interview with good inter-rater agreement. Median percentages of agreement ranged from 72 percent (open-ended questions and paraphrases) to 100 percent (reflections of feelings and summarizations). With each statement thus identified, it became possible to compare the specific responses of the experimental and control group. In future research, it should be possible to use this same method to determine the effectiveness of varying responses on different clients. It may be anticipated that certain specific distributions of counselor statements are more effective with varying types of clients. The microtraining framework coupled with Moreland's straightforward method of classifying interview responses may result in an increased understanding of client-counselor interaction patterns in the interview.

SUMMARY

The three studies summarized here are helpful, as they further illustrate the diversity of questions that can be answered by research utilizing the microtraining paradigm. They illustrate the feasibility of applying the microtraining format to issues as varying as behavioral counts of eye contact breaks, generalization of a single behavior to a classroom setting, and generalization of several behaviors to the therapeutic session.

Work with microtraining seems constantly to provide more questions for further examination than it answers. It may be suggested that the microtraining format is a suitable one for finding both new answers and new questions.

REFERENCES

Aldrige, E.: The Microtraining Paradigm in the Instruction of Junior High School Students in Attending Behavior. Unpublished dissertation, Amherst, University of Massachusetts, 1971.

Moreland, J.: Video Programmed Instruction in Elementary Psychotherapeutic and Related Clinical Skills. Unpublished dissertation, Amherst, University of Massachusetts, 1971.

Sadker, M.: Modification of the Frequency of Student-Initiated Higher-Order Questions Through Microteaching and a Token Economy. Unpublished dissertation, Amherst, University of Massachusetts, 1971.

NAME INDEX

199

SUBJECT INDEX

A

Affectivity-sensitivity scale, 114
Applications of microcounseling
client training, 82, 100-101
co-counseling supervision, 102
college undergraduate course, 104-105
community youth programs, 99-100
comprehensive approach to single interview, 103-104
counseling and therapy training laboratories, 176-180
drug counselors, 107-108
large groups, 106
marital communication, 107
mental patients, 94-95, 121
paraprofessionals, 23-24, 32, 78, 95-96, 117
preparation for job interviews, 96-97
self-understanding workshops, 97-99
social work training, 106
speech pathology, 107
teacher aides, 107
teacher training, 89-91
teaching human relations skills, xii, 91-92, 132-134
teaching junior high students, 106, *also see* Appendix C
teaching students skills of being students, 93-94, *also see* Appendix C
Attending behavior, vii, xii, 30-33, 35 fn., 52-54, 79, 100, 148, 149-150, 185-190, *also see* Appendix C
Attention, 37 fn.
Attention and
attending behavior, 38-41
autogenic training, 48
behavioral components, 37-41
existentialism, 48-49

hypnosis, 48
memory, 48
reinforcement, 37-38
Zen, 48
Audiotapes in counselor training, 19, 114, 122, 124

B

Behavioral counts, 114, 116-118, 120, *also see* Appendix C
Behavioral objectives curriculum, 91-92, 132-134
Behavioral repertoire, viii, 28-29, 45-46, 113
Behavioral skills, identification of, 78-80, 110
Body movement, *see* Nonverbal communication

C

Checklist of Therapist Errors, 27-29, 114, 116-117
Client training prior to counseling, 82, 100-101
Clients in microtraining, 80-82, 87-88
Co-counseling supervision, 102
College teaching (ways to improve), 89-91, 93-94
College undergraduate courses, 104-105
Community youth programs, 99-100
Component skills approach, *see* Single skills approach
Counseling and therapy training laboratories, 176-180
Counselor Effectiveness Scale, 31, 119, 174-184

203